A Higher Education

A Higher Education
Baylor and the Vocation of a Christian University

edited by

Elizabeth Davis

BAYLOR UNIVERSITY PRESS

© 2012 by Baylor University Press
Waco, Texas 76798-7363

All Rights Reserved. No part of this publication may be reproduced, stored in a retrieval system, or transmitted, in any form or by any means, electronic, mechanical, photocopying, recording, or otherwise, without the prior permission in writing of Baylor University Press.

Cover Design by Cynthia Dunne, Blue Farm Graphics
Cover Image: Baylor University Seal © Baylor University. Used by permission.

Library of Congress Cataloging-in-Publication Data

A Higher Education : Baylor and the vocation of a Christian university / edited by Elizabeth Davis.
 125 p. cm.
 Includes bibliographical references.
 ISBN 978-1-60258-681-9 (hardback : alk. paper)
 1. Church and college—United States. 2. Christian universities and colleges—United States. 3. Education, Higher—Aims and objectives—United States. 4. Baylor University. I. Davis, Elizabeth, 1962–
 LC383.B35 2012
 378'.071—dc23
                    2012032067

The paperback ISBN for this title is 978-1-4813-0329-3.
First paperback printing, 2014.

Printed in the United States of America on acid-free paper.

TABLE OF CONTENTS

Foreword *Kenneth Winston Starr*		vii
Introduction: Why Christian Higher Education Matters *Elizabeth Davis*		1
1	Christian Higher Education vs. Christians in Higher Education *Kenneth G. Elzinga*	7
2	The Myth of the Sovereign Self *Jean Bethke Elshtain*	21
3	Scholarship in Action and the Public Mission of Universities *Nancy Cantor*	35
4	Ethics in the Twenty-First Century *Baruch A. Brody*	53
5	The Challenges and Opportunities for Liberal Education in a Faith-Based University *Lee S. Shulman*	75
6	The Bible, Baptists, and the Challenge of Christian Higher Education *Mark Noll*	95
Notes		113

FOREWORD

— *Kenneth Winston Starr* —

President, Baylor University

When I was invited to serve as the fourteenth President of Baylor University, the world of higher education was—and continues to be—in a state of flux. Tuition costs for any university—nearly without exception—are rising steadily. New theories about how a university is and ought to be run are being tried and tested. Luckily, conversations focused on determining the real aim of higher education are bringing to light what a complex and even confusing field this can be.

It was also a critical point in Baylor's history as our 2012 strategic plan began drawing to a close. Looking back, the Baylor family was obligated to ask whether we were tracking to accomplish all we had set out to do in 2002 when the twelve imperatives of Baylor 2012 were fashioned. However, our perspective was Janusian, for as we looked into the past to measure our progress, we looked also to the future and saw another basic question taking shape: "what next?"

As we prepared to launch into the creation of this next chapter in Baylor history, it was critical that we begin with the appropriate tone. These inaugural speeches were intended as catalysts—insights and perspectives that would spark numerous campus conversations as we look forward. The series was intended to bring a group of outstanding thinkers and scholars well versed in the world of higher education to Baylor to enrich our discussion as we plan our next steps. We invited these outstanding men and women to campus so that their words would in turn invite and challenge the Baylor faculty, staff, and students to be a part of this large conversation—to take ownership of their school and the direction we take as 2012 draws to a close.

We are recalibrating—setting a new trajectory for Baylor in the ever-changing world of higher education. The Board of Regents and I firmly agreed that the goals we set for ourselves be determined not by the understandably limited perspective of any one person or group. The vision would have to be a composite drawn even from the far reaches of the Baylor family and the entire Christian community.

As you read these speeches, know that the conversation continues. As we prepare for a new phase in Baylor history, we are mapping out the next leg of an unfolding journey, framing the history of Baylor, the twenty-first century University. We are embarking on many exciting new endeavors already, and the pace only quickens. So as we sculpt Baylor's future, I invite you to pick up a chisel and add your voice to the conversation. The future of Baylor belongs to all of us. May the thoughts contained in this book inspire us to be good stewards of Baylor's future.

INTRODUCTION
Why Christian Higher Education Matters

— *Elizabeth Davis* —

Provost, Baylor University

In the last decade America has experienced the unprecedented horrors of 9/11 and endured two wars, costly in both treasure and blood. We've been rocked by the bursting of the housing bubble and a double-dip recession. In 2010 over 46 million Americans lived below the official poverty line, the highest count in the 52 years since the Census Bureau started tracking such figures.[1] Looming on the horizon are the emerging giants India, China, and Brazil, whose economic appetites, many predict, will displace America from her role as the world's economic and political superpower.[2] America faces an uncertain future in which the American dream may indeed be just a dream.

America's colleges and universities have proven themselves time and again a critical and resilient resource in the challenge of making and re-making America. Education was present at the very start of American history. The colonies needed cultural capital, and the founders, rich in wisdom and foresight, established colleges to provide what the fledgling colonies needed most—clergy, lawyers, and leaders. The wisdom and courage essential after the Revolution were manifested in the graduates of our young country's colleges. The architects of the American experiment were trained by America's colleges. During America's greatest identity crisis—when we as a nation were deciding on whether we were one, equal and free, or whether we were many, stratified and subjugated—an American president, again rich in wisdom and foresight, proposed legislation that gave birth to America's flagship land grant institutions. And it was America's institutions of higher education that threw open their doors to educate a whole generation at the end of WWII.[3]

Traditional higher education is still seen as the best way to improve one's lot in life even in today's troubled times. Michael Greenstone and Adam Looney of the Brookings Institution have demonstrated that the average earning differential generated by a $102,000 investment in a college degree provides a return that beats 30-year average returns in the stock market, or in gold, long-term bonds, or home ownership.[4] It is no wonder then that the prevailing rhetoric in Washington, D.C. is for a greater proportion of the citizenry to have a post-secondary degree, not only to improve lives individually, but to enhance the country's economic position internationally.

Despite being a constant and sustaining resource for America, higher education has historically been a target for criticism. In 1934 a writer in the *Journal of Higher Education* summarized the view of critics as follows:

> They say that our universities are aimless institutions that have prostituted themselves to every public whim, serving as everything from a reformatory to an amusement park; they are . . . presided over by quacks. . . . The trustees . . . are men entirely unfitted for their tasks, ridiculously conservative and fearful, controlled body and soul by Wall Street. The presidents are liars and hypocrites, academic Machiavellis, who dull the intellectual life of the colleges, cow the faculties, and stultify the student body. . . . The faculty members are weak, cringing creatures . . . not one of them would trust himself to earn even a poor livelihood in the outside world.[5]

Criticism of higher education is nothing new, and neither is the application of business models to higher education. The "business" of higher education began early in the twentieth century with the rapid rise of industrialization. But the phenomenal growth of the corporate "for profit" universities has brought a greater and more focused pressure upon all institutions. The expectation is that higher education should become more like businesses, or at a minimum be run and judged like a business.[6]

Ironically, though, to run a university like a business could force all institutions, whether public or private, to become just like each other. Individual pursuit of the common goals of efficiency, service, and profitability could lead to conformity. Such conformity would diminish the educational landscape—moving American universities to a single model system would result in a loss of the richness of our current system, one that caters to differing student needs and expectations.

On one end of the spectrum are the for-profit colleges, community colleges, and many of the online degree programs offered by traditional universities. These colleges and programs target students who cannot participate in a traditional college experience but who want and need courses available at times and in formats that fit their schedules. At the other end of the spectrum are the most elite private colleges, the most successful flagship public universities, and other institutions with sterling reputations. At these institutions, the demand for a brand-name degree and the traditional residential student model will remain higher than the supply. Elite private institutions, in particular, will deliberately *not* meet demand; that is, they will not grow to the equilibrium point where supply and demand are equal at a particular tuition or price level because of the perceived connection between exclusivity and elite status. Spread across the middle of the spectrum are public and private institutions with less-known identities. These institutions have been able to maintain a consistent influx of students because the population of 18- to 24-year-olds has been growing for decades. However, colleges and universities operating in the middle will not be able to survive as they are currently configured. According to Moody's 2011 Outlook for U.S. Higher Education, market shifts favor the lowest cost or the highest reputation competitors.[7] Institutions in the middle will face intense pressure to move toward the endpoints and compete for students.

The world needs major comprehensive universities, like Baylor, that are informed and shaped by a Christian worldview. While critics decry the status of higher education from a cost and efficiency point of view, others are taking the academic world to task for abandoning an original obligation for the moral formation of America's youth. In his book *Education's End: Why Our Colleges and Universities Have Given*

Up on the Meaning of Life, Yale law professor Anthony T. Kronman laments that life's purpose and meaning have lost status as legitimate subjects of discussion and debate within the ivy-covered walls of colleges and universities. Academia has abandoned to churches its responsibility to struggle with these issues.[8]

Baylor clearly does not aspire to be one of the mass providers, but instead to offer a distinctive education. But this claim does beg the question, "What unique position does Baylor fill such that, if Baylor were to disappear, its unique role could not be filled by any other institution in the ecology of higher education?"[9]

The following chapters in this volume—addresses delivered to the faculty, staff, and students of Baylor University, celebrating the inauguration of Kenneth Winston Starr as Baylor's President—will suggest something of the exceptional vocational mission of Baylor. Ken Elzinga (University of Virginia) outlines the distinctive role of a Christian university within the academy. Jean Bethke Elshtain (University of Chicago) provides a warning about the myth of the sovereign self in liberal education, before offering the cure of sacrifice and service to others. Nancy Cantor (Syracuse University) challenges Baylor to fulfill her mission of "Pro Texana" by enacting scholarship. Baruch Brody (Rice University) confronts the ethical issues arising from a Christian university's discovery and application of new knowledge. Lee Shulman (Stanford University) dispels often assumed contradictions between an education that is liberal and one that is Christian. Finally, Mark Noll (Notre Dame) discusses the challenges of Baylor's historic Baptist identity, with its commitments to the Bible as Scripture, in the context of higher education.

Baylor University strives to stand in a place occupied by few other institutions—set apart by an unwavering Christian identity, an enduring dedication to transformative education, and a strong and growing commitment to research. Over the course of the nineteenth and twentieth centuries, a relentless retreat transpired from Christian commitment on the part of the nation's oldest and most prestigious universities. Baylor, however, has persisted in the belief that not only can its Baptist heritage inform a vital approach to life in general, but it can also inform the life of the mind specifically. We hold firm to the conviction that the world needs a preeminent research university that is unambiguously Christian. A place where such a commitment does not imply a lack of scholarly inquiry, but rather requires scholarship and creative endeavors at the highest levels of quality to complement and inform its teaching and service. It is hoped that this volume can help this university and others see Baylor's unique calling and why Christian higher education matters.

1

CHRISTIAN HIGHER EDUCATION VS. CHRISTIANS IN HIGHER EDUCATION

— Kenneth G. Elzinga —

Robert C. Taylor Professor of Economics, University of Virginia

It is a custom for public speakers in the U.S. to say, "I'm glad to be here." Usually that statement is a total fabrication. The speaker would rather be at the beach, at a concert, or at home reading a book. But in my case, I am happy to be here. It also is an honor for me to speak at Baylor University in conjunction with Ken Starr assuming the presidency of this institution.

Economists are not always known for the accuracy of their forecasts. But I predict that Baylor University will flourish under President Starr's leadership. As an aside, I have long had an affection for Baylor University, in no small part because one of its faculty, Professor Joe McKinney, profoundly influenced and shaped my own personal and professional life. And it is a privilege for me to speak about a topic that goes right to the heart of this institution's future as a university with a Christian identity.

I want to distinguish Christian higher education from Christians in higher education.

Let me begin, if I may, on an autobiographical note. I joined the faculty of the University of Virginia in the fall of 1967, as a freshly minted Ph.D. I'll let you do the arithmetic if you want to estimate how old I am.

For all of my career, except for two semesters, I have been a faculty member at secular schools. The University of Virginia is often called "Mr. Jefferson's university" because Thomas Jefferson conceived and designed the school. The institution is relentlessly secular, as Mr. Jefferson would have wanted: Thomas Jefferson, after all, is the founding father most identified with the constitutional doctrine of a separation between church and state.

What does it mean for a school to be relentlessly secular? Try these on for size.

When I arrived at UVA in 1967, Christian student groups were not permitted to meet on the grounds of the University. So far as I know, Virginia was the only public university to have this restraint. How God used two UVA students to break down this barrier is a story worth telling, but not here.

As an assistant professor, I once tried to schedule a room in the student union for a faculty Bible study and was told no. I asked if I could schedule a room to discuss the writings of Karl Marx. No problem. To read *Mein Kampf*? Not an eyebrow was raised. But the gospel of Mark—that was apparently off limits to discuss on grounds.

I'm happy to report that these situations have changed. But if Mr. Jefferson were to return to the grounds of his university today, he would not find any "establishment," (to use his word), much less promotion, of religious faith.

Now let me tell you one more autobiographical fact, perhaps relevant to this talk. When parents ask me to speak to their high school age children about attending the University of Virginia, if in the course of the conversation I learn that the children are followers of Jesus, I ask them if they are considering a Christian school as well. And if not, I ask why. And we have a conversation about the costs and benefits (remember, I'm an economist) of Christian versus secular schools.

I am a friend of Christian higher education even though my calling, as a matter of vocation, has been to a secular school.

That is the personal background I bring to the question: what is the difference between *Christians in higher education* and *Christian higher education*?

Let me begin with taxonomy. At secular schools, Christians in higher education can be placed into two different bins or categories.

I'm not happy with the terms, but I'll call one group the "privatizers" and the other the "evangelicals."

Privatizers in higher education are dualists. Another term for them might be "two-spheres Christians." Privatizers (or two-spheres Christians) view their faith as disconnected from their work as professors. They may be involved in a local church (often heavily involved). But these professors, the privatizers, are not identified at their schools as Christians; this aspect of their identity may never be known by students or colleagues.

It is not that their faith is a deep or dark secret; they simply consider this data point about themselves irrelevant to their life in the academy. They are identified as professors of chemistry or accounting or German literature. Their Christian faith is private and apart from their jobs.

These professors live in two worlds, not simultaneously, but sequentially: one is secular, their campus; the other is sacred, their church.

Now let me say, as an aside, that from my observation some Christian faculty at Christian colleges and universities live like privatizers as well.

The second kind of Christian professor in secular higher education I'll call the evangelical. The term "evangelical" is a portmanteau expression and requires some unpacking. I do not mean it as a simple label. By evangelical I mean to include all those—Catholic, Orthodox, and Protestant—who subscribe warmly to the biblical and theological tenets of the Christian church, those cardinal beliefs and affirmations that have been reiterated in the confessions and creedal affirmation of our churches.

The professors, researchers, and scholars in higher education whom I have labeled the evangelicals believe that the quest for truth begins and ends with Jesus. Their work involves teaching and research in their disciplines. But their calling entails extending the reign of Jesus into all realms.

The evangelicals resonate with the words of the Dutch Reformer Abraham Kuyper: "There is not one square inch of the entire creation about which Jesus Christ does not cry out, 'This is mine! This belongs to me.'"[1] They are professors who, in accord with I Peter 3:15, are "always ready to give a defense of the hope that is within them," but they do so, as the Apostle Peter also makes clear, "with gentleness and reverence."[2]

You will *not* find these professors praying before class; you will *not* find these professors proclaiming the gospel in the classroom; you will *not* find these professors teaching their courses from a "Christian perspective." While they are Christians in higher education, their institutional environment is not one of Christian higher education. Their lectures will not begin with a prayer nor will they end with an altar call.

Indeed, evangelicals at secular schools must be scrupulously fair and impartial with their students who are not followers of Jesus, treating the academic endeavors of these students in the same way they would those students who share their Christian convictions.

Evangelical professors may be quite visible as Christians at their secular colleges and universities. But they operate under the constraint that, fundamentally, they have been hired by their institutions to teach and do research in a particular discipline or subject matter, not to evangelize or engage in gospel proclamation.

To the extent that they are open about their Christian faith, the evangelicals discuss it with students in the same way that professors who are enthused about activities like sailing or cooking might share their interests. A professor who is passionate about sailing can make that known to her students; her students in turn may find that interesting and may even take up sailing themselves. But all her students understand that an interest or disinterest in sailing has nothing to do with the treatment the student receives in the classroom or laboratory. Students of an evangelical professor in higher education understand that their grade is not a function of their own religious beliefs, or lack thereof.

Robert Benchley once observed, "There are two kinds of people in the world: those who divide the world into two kinds of people, and those who don't."[3] For purposes of this talk, I am in the first group. In my reductionist, bimodal distribution, one Christian professor sees his faith as largely irrelevant to his job. The other sees her job as a calling under the lordship of Jesus. No doubt there are Christian faculty who manage to straddle the bimodal distribution. But my reductionism is useful for where I am going next.

Now let me turn to Christian higher education. What should it look like? To contextualize the question, what should Baylor University be like, compared to an institution like the University of Virginia? How should the two schools differ? What is the difference between my being a Christian in higher education and a school like Baylor actually doing or producing or being Christian higher education?

Here is my understanding of Christian higher education.

Christian higher education does not start with Christian students. That surprises some of my colleagues at UVA. Some Christian colleges and universities have a Christian litmus test for the enrolling of students. Such a requirement is a distraction.

If prospective students who are academically qualified want to be a part of Christian higher education, they should be welcome. If the Christian faith is defensible, if the Christian faith is compelling, if the Christian faith is true, non-Christian students should be welcome to live and learn in the environment of Christian higher education and test the faith.

Just as Jesus did not throw out Doubting Thomas, Christian higher education should be an environment that welcomes Doubting Thomases, as students.

But Christian higher education, to merit that designation and imprimatur, should be dominated by a faculty who are followers of Jesus. By that I mean the majority of faculty at an institution of Christian higher education should be Christians. The designation or description makes no sense if that is not the case.

It is not my job—it might be President Starr's—to determine precisely what constitutes a majority. And it is not my job—it might be President Starr's—to determine the taxonomy of the term "Christian." But I shall suggest a minimal hurdle or benchmark (that I first heard from David Bast): faculty members who can agree to the Nicene Creed without crossing their fingers behind their backs. I realize this benchmark may not square with the Baptist motto "no creed but the Bible." My point here is not to spotlight the Nicene Creed, but rather to make a point about the relevance and importance of some defining taxonomy.

Regarding Christian higher education, R. R. Reno recently wrote,

> Not every professor and graduate student must be Christian. Not all scholarship has to crackle with the ardor of faith. Committed Jewish or Muslim or Hindu scholars can contribute to a spirit of faithful inquiry at a Christian school. In fact, their witness in our contemporary academic culture on antinomianism and unbelief can be far more powerful than the example of a Christian scholar who bows to the latest academic fashions.[4]

Students are transients; they come and go. Christian higher education is defined by a core of faculty who believe that Jesus is the way, the truth, and the life (John 14:16), and that every thought is to be made captive to Him—and they, the faculty, are not ashamed of the gospel.

My undergraduate school was begun by Baptists many years ago. I have no doubt that the founders of that college were committed Christians who had a vision for a school that would embody Christian higher education. Over the years, the influence of Christianity waned at that school, as it has at so many colleges and universities in the United States.

When I was an undergraduate, I remember the college president stating that the school had hired its first avowed atheist on the faculty. This was announced with a measure of pride, as if the institution had become of age.

For those who would object, arguing that requiring a faculty body that is predominantly Christian will suppress otherwise unfettered academic freedom of inquiry and the pursuit of truth, I would respond in two ways. The first is a request to consider how secular institutions have suppressed unfettered academic freedom as well. The second is a rhetorical question: if Christian higher education is not made so by Christian educators, what is the alternative paradigm that merits the label?

So Christian higher education starts with Christian faculty.

Christian higher education also will have rules and precepts for living in a Christian community. But the rules are derivative of Christian higher education; they are not the foundation.

Years ago, T. S. Eliot put the matter this way: "The purpose of Christian higher education would not be merely to make men and women pious Christians . . . A Christian education must primarily teach people to be able to think in Christian categories."⁵

On this point, I have a different view from that of many parents as to why their children should be at schools like Baylor University. I know parents who want their children to go to a school with Christian roots and a continuing Christian identity because they think their children are less likely to get involved in drugs, less likely to get AIDS, less likely to fall in love with a non-Christian, less likely to . . . well, it's a long list—but the list goes right down to less likely to end up wearing a ring in their nose or having a tattoo on their neck.

I do not make light of these parental concerns. But my concept of Christian higher education travels in a different direction than rules of student conduct. I happen not to think that Christian higher education should be safe. I think Christian higher education should have an edge to it, just as it was dangerous to hang around with Jesus and even riskier to follow Him.

Christian higher education should be defined by differences in *teaching*, differences in *credentialing*, and differences in *mentoring*. The faculty are pivotal in each of these.

Let me say as an aside that, if I had time for another talk, I would discuss how Christian higher education might cause differences in curriculum, tuition, and even the campus bookstore.

I mention all these because the difference between Christians in higher education and Christian higher education is not minor or cosmetic. Christian higher education should be radically different. And if my French were better, I would say, vive la différence.

Let me allocate five minutes on teaching, five minutes on credentialing, five minutes on mentoring, and five minutes to conclude.

Teaching

It probably goes without saying that when a physicist at Baylor University teaches Bernoulli's theorem, it is not taught differently from the way it would be taught at UVA. When I teach the economic principle of demand elasticity at UVA, I am confident the identical formula is taught by Professor McKinney and his colleagues here at Baylor. Ricardo's principle of comparative advantage shows the same benefits of free trade when taught in Charlottesville that it does in Waco.

But when I teach the economic theory of income distribution at the University of Virginia, it is not fair game for me to ask what the biblical principle of gleaning—leaving some extra grain in the fields for the poor—might teach about income distribution in an industrialized society.

One can have this kind of conversation in Christian higher education. It should not be out of bounds to consider biblical perspectives in Christian higher education even if Christians in higher education who are at secular schools cannot readily go there.

This is called integration: integrating the Christian faith with one's discipline. It is not easy to do. And it will involve different shapes and forms in different disciplines to take the Bible's great themes of creation, fall, and redemption and weave them into classroom discourse.

To my mind, this is a primary distinction between Christian higher education and Christians in higher education. The classrooms and laboratories and seminar rooms of Christian higher education are places where faculty and students are free to explore topics that may be off-limits to Christian faculty at secular universities or universities where such themes are simply irrelevant to the academic discourse.

If the faculty members in Christian higher education simply believe their job is to teach what they learned in graduate school and then go home and be good church members, integration won't take place. And the school will produce a generation of students of which many will come to believe that there is a gap (if not a chasm) between the secular and the sacred.

Joel Carpenter has written that every Christian school needs some faculty "who focus on questions of faith and knowledge and a Christian worldview," but goes on to add that in Christian higher education "[e]very professor must in some sense be a lay theologian."[6]

Professor Perry L. Glanzer is on the faculty at Baylor. His article on redemptive moral development in higher education is the best paper I know on the subject.[7]

I find it difficult to improve upon his proposal:

> I believe Christian colleges, such as my own, should rename their religion departments as theology departments in order to highlight the fact that we seek to help students become worshipping theologians versed in the narratives, affections and practices of the

Church and not merely critical thinkers about religion. General education courses pertaining to Bible or theology could also use this reorienting... Beyond theology, a Christian liberal education should both deepen our understanding of Christian practices and help us think critically about them.[8]

CREDENTIALS

Now let me turn to credentialing. And what I am trying to say here is awkward for me to explain. Let me start this way. The business world emphasizes credentials. The professions of law and medicine emphasize credentials. But higher education *really* emphasizes credentials. We put them before our names, after our names; we calibrate and quantify performance; we rank people all the time; we look up to and look down on people according to performance-based credentials or titles.

For years I wrote a personal letter of congratulations to every student of mine who got an A+. I was proud of them. They made me look good too. I still do this, but now I write a letter to every student who fails my classes. Last fall I wrote twenty of those letters.

I suspect Jesus would have thought first to write the F students. Christian higher education would recognize (before I did) that the A+ students already get lots of strokes. It took me about twenty years to catch on to writing the young men and women who failed my class, and whom, perhaps, I had failed as their teacher.

De-emphasizing credentials is a mark of Christian higher education. I am much taken by the Apostle Paul's example here.

How does Paul generally state his credentials? Right at the front of his epistles. Read the first verse of Romans, "Paul, a servant of Christ Jesus"; Philippians 1:1, "Paul and Timothy, servants of Christ Jesus"; Titus 1:1, "Paul, a servant of God and an apostle of Jesus Christ." In most of higher education, "a servant" is not much of a credential. It should be in Christian higher education.

I consider credentialing one of the most important areas of distinction between Christian higher education and secular schools.[9]

Let me be as clear as I know how: as a fan of Baylor University, I am pleased to learn when her students get into Ivy League schools to do graduate work. But because what Baylor University is about is *Christian* higher education, I also am pleased to learn when Baylor students who were estranged from their families have been reconciled as a consequence of being in this academic community,

and that some Baylor students who came to Waco shackled by materialism are free of those bonds when they leave,

and that some Baylor students who were chronically dishonest upon their arrival now let their "yea be yea" and their "nay be nay,"

and that some Baylor students who once were snobs now are marked by humility because of being part of this academic community,

and that some Baylor students who once believed that the world is really nothing more than a random collocation of atoms in a purposeless universe now realize that they are made in God's image and that the whole world is full of God's glory.

Baylor University can place an advertisement in the *Chronicle of Higher Education* heralding the number of its students who go on to do graduate work in the Ivy League. That's easy to do. But somehow, Baylor also needs to recognize and acknowledge to its constituents that the very best students here are the sanctified ones, the broken ones, whom God can use. Precisely how Christian higher education can encourage and commend sanctification without it becoming a line item on a student's résumé will be an unending challenge.

Professors play a role here. Students in Christian higher education need to know that the faculty value the character and moral compass of their students: that professors admire godliness; that the faculty's deepest satisfaction as professors comes from seeing students become what God wants them to be—people for whom Jesus Christ is preeminent.

Mentoring

Now let me talk about mentoring (or discipling).

I would expect Christian higher education to be characterized by professors who mentor students. Not just teach them chemistry and accounting, not just teach them biology and Spanish, but model for them how to walk with Jesus; not because these faculty members have mastered how to do this, but because they have been pilgrims longer and because they have more experience with the consequences of sin and redemption.

I have been surprised, in my travels, at how few faculty members in Christian higher education mentor or disciple students. When I have asked why, the answer I sometimes hear is, that's for the Dean of the Chapel to do, or that's the job of the Dean of Students' office.

I am an economist, so I understand that answer. It is right out of Adam Smith; it appeals to what Adam Smith called specialization and division of labor.

But while I understand the answer, I can restrain my enthusiasm for it. To me, it means that Christian higher education has professors who are not investing in the lives of students beyond teaching them chemistry and accounting and biology and Spanish.

But you can learn chemistry and accounting and biology and Spanish anywhere; and often at less cost than in Christian higher education.

Many institutions of higher education in the United States, which effectively and productively insert faculty into classroom and laboratory settings for teaching purposes, struggle to use the same faculty to advise students outside the classroom and laboratory. The *Chronicle of Higher Education* recently ran an article by Mark Montgomery at Grinnell College entitled "Confessions of a Bad Academic Advisor."[10] Most faculty members I know can relate to that article. It can be difficult and awkward, whether the professor is at a secular school or a Christian school, to advise a first-year student as to exactly which level of calculus or Spanish class is optimal, much less advise a student on whether they ought to pursue a career in teaching or health care instead of commerce or state government.

But Christian higher education exists because there once was a Galilean who made disciples. His disciples called Him Rabbi, or teacher. And therein lies a principle by which teachers today are to invite—not coerce, but invite—students to be their disciples, that is, to mentor them. Jesus taught His followers the Law and the Prophets. But He also lived among them and even washed their feet. I have often wondered what the Lord's illustration of foot washing means to the professoriate of the 21st century.

I once tried to refill the water glass of an international student who was a dinner guest in my home. "No, no," he said. "You are the professor; I cannot let you serve me. In my country, it is the other way around." My initial thought was, that sounds like a nice place to be a professor!

But as a Christian professor, I am asked to think through what it means to be a foot-washer. Many of my students would not want their feet washed, and many do not want to be discipled. But in Christian higher education, there should be students who learn more than the material in the textbook and lecture, because they are in an institution that values—that is, it devotes resources to—the making and forming of disciples.

Conclusion

I look at my notes and see that I am nearing the end of my talk. When I was in college, my speech teacher told me that I should always inform my audience when I was nearing the end of a talk. She told me it would revive hope among my audience.

At the risk of sounding obsequious, let me mention that Baylor University gets a lot of things right in modeling Christian higher education.

Christian professors at secular schools would look with envy (sanctified envy, I would hope) at Baylor's sponsorship of a conference like "The King James Bible and the World It Made" that assembles scholars like Philip Jenkins, Alister McGrath, Mark Noll, Lamin Sanneh, Robert Alter, David Bebbington, Laura Knoppers, and N. T. Wright under one roof; or Baylor's symposium on "Sacred Texts, Holy Images," with exhibitions of Chagall, Rouault, and Fujimura. Baylor University's Institute for Studies of Religion is internationally known. In my own field of economics, some of the premier conferences linking the dismal science and the Christian faith have been on this campus.

In short, there is a great foundation already established at this institution. If I may take a certain liberty with the words of the Apostle Paul, in his first letter to the Thessalonians, he commended Christians in Thessalonica for their sanctification, but then wrote, "we urge and exhort you in the Lord Jesus that you should abound *more and more* . . ." (I Thess. 4:1), and soon thereafter, after commending them for their brotherly love, Paul writes, "we urge you, brethren, that you increase *more and more* . . ." (I Thess. 4:10).

To put Paul's words in an academic context, as Baylor University seeks to fulfill its mission of offering Christian higher education, in the midst of its current track record, may the school's trajectory be one of "more and more."

When Jesus claims to be the way, the truth, and the life, He honors truth. Christian higher education honors the pursuit of truth in the natural sciences, the social sciences, the humanities, the applied sciences, the professions, and the arts. The pursuit of Christian higher education elevates students and professors as well, by giving them the lofty status of being made in God's image. Secular universities can tell their students nothing more than that they are the best and the brightest.

President Starr has explained his understanding of the pursuit of truth with the expression "discovery of new knowledge." Mr. Jefferson, the founder of the University of Virginia, would agree with that. But President Starr does not stop there.

In the most recent issue of *First Things*, he wrote:

> One of Baylor's core convictions is to "facilitate the discovery of new knowledge *to the glory of God* and the betterment of humanity." . . . Baylor is a place where, at our best, we develop the manifold gifts of body, mind, and spirit and, by doing so, seek to *glorify the creator* whose handiwork we are and whose creation we study and celebrate.[11]

My own theological convictions have been influenced by the Protestant Reformation. Consequently, I am struck by how my aspirations for Baylor University under President Starr's leadership line up with what Reverend John Jenkins said in his inaugural address as the new president of Notre Dame. These are Jenkins' words:

> Notre Dame is different. Combining religious faith and academic excellence is not widely emulated or even admired among the opinion-makers in higher education. Yet, in this age especially, we at Notre Dame must have the courage to be who we are. If we are afraid to be different from the world, how can we make a difference in the world?[12]

Let me swap just a couple of words and geographically transfer what President Jenkins said from Indiana to Texas, from Hoosier country to the Lone Star State:

> Baylor University is different. Combining religious faith and academic excellence is not widely emulated or even admired among the

opinion-makers in higher education. Yet, in this age especially, we at Baylor University must have the courage to be who we are. If we are afraid to be different from the world, how can we make a difference in the world?

The opening line of C. S. Lewis' *The Voyage of the Dawn Treader* is "There was a boy called Eustace Clarence Scrubb, and he almost deserved it." Isn't that a wonderful opening line? That opening line, with the name Eustace Clarence Scrubb, doesn't match Melville's opening line "Call me Ishmael" in *Moby Dick*, but it comes close. Of this boy, Lewis wrote, "Although [Eustace] didn't care much about any subject for its own sake, he cared a great deal about [grades]." Secular schools have a difficult time explaining why students should care about a subject for its own sake. But Christian higher education can explain this quite readily. Thank God—quite literally—for that.

From an economist's perspective, Christian higher education also expands the choice set of higher education. Baylor University makes for a more diverse population of educational inputs and outputs. Even students at schools of Christian higher education who are not themselves followers of Jesus ought to support the Christian distinctives of their schools, if only because of the valuable diversity schools like Baylor bring to American higher education.

Such diversity reminds me of Benjamin Franklin's remark at the close of the Constitutional Convention in 1787, when he said, "We have given you a republic, if you can keep it."

One hundred and sixty five years ago, if I did my arithmetic correctly, the founders of Baylor University, in effect, said: "we have given you an institution of Christian higher education, if you can keep it." One hundred and sixty-five years later, Baylor University's homepage describes the school as a "Christian community of faith." President Starr, trustees, and faculty, you have been given an institution of Christian higher education. May you continue to keep it until the Lord Jesus returns.

2

THE MYTH OF THE SOVEREIGN SELF

— Jean Bethke Elshtain —

Laura Spelman Rockefeller Professor of Social and Political Ethics
in the Divinity School, Department of Political Science and the Committee
on International Relations, University of Chicago

I will offer some general comments about the liberal arts and the humanities, and then go on to talk about a specific manifestation of modernity, and the way in which what we might call a classical education or a liberal arts education might help to inform and illumine us as we reflect on the tumult of our time.

From time to time there is a flurry of excitement concerning the future of the humanities and liberal arts education. The general tone is one of urgency. We're told that we neglect the humanities at our peril; if we lose our liberal arts heritage, our entire cultural identity is jeopardized, and so on.

There is of course great truth to these kinds of claims. But some defenders of liberal education go much further and make rather grand if not grandiose pronouncements. In a sense, they instrumentalize liberal education. Reading the classics, we are told, will make us better men and women. Those trained in liberal education will be more open to "the other" and less ethnocentric. They will be good citizens. This is often topped off by the insistence that the humanities alone instill what is called "critical thinking," and that those bereft of such an education will more likely be uncritically conformist to the terms of their own society, whatever those terms may be.

Unfortunately, this set of grand claims in behalf of liberal education does not bear up under critical scrutiny, at least not in the way its defenders proclaim. Let me take a historical example. Germany in the twentieth century was the most literate country in Europe—the great classics were studied, the great music was played—and this did nothing to prevent the rise and eventual triumph of Fascism; it did nothing to guarantee better people. We all know of the classical music performed by death camp inmates who were spared temporarily because of their musical abilities as tens of thousands marched to their deaths in the crematoria. Hitler's highest aspiration—indeed his obsession—was to build a great cultural center in the new Europe, the new Nazified Europe, replete with art museums, the greatest opera house ever known, the most beautiful buildings ever seen.

Upon entering occupied Paris, the first thing Hitler did was to go to the Paris opera house in order to assess the acoustics because he wanted to create a glorious opera house in his cultural center. Invading Germans, under orders, seized great works of art, all over Europe, from private and public collections, and their intended new home was to be one of several art museums being built in this grandiose new site.

We see too readily how the most brutish barbarism and the arts and humanities can somehow coexist. And we also know something else about this terrible period of time. We know that rescuers, those who risked their lives to save Jews and others marked for destruction, included both the well educated and the illiterate. What these brave souls had in common was not a liberal education, but rather a faith. Religious conviction did not guarantee that one would be a rescuer, that one would join those ranks, but without that faith it was a near certainty that one would not extend oneself in this way. In other words, we should not look to the liberal arts to save us, or anybody else. For that, we must seek elsewhere. But can the humanities—even if they can't "save us," as some seem to suggest—illumine, can they teach, can they sustain in some powerful ways?

To complicate things a bit further, it is worth noting that altogether too many of our departments in the humanities in higher education today, in major research institutions in the United States and Europe, have, in the words of one contemporary critic, "disgraced themselves" by treating revered works of art and literature with disdain. One doesn't read seriously the great works, because they allegedly represent the debris of the past. I submit that this pridefulness, the idea that what's gone before cannot instruct us, is not an example of critical thinking so much as not thinking at all. In order to criticize a tradition, you need to know it and understand it first.

Now, it seems that I should depart the stage posthaste, for I appear to have ripped the ground out from under that which I'm here to talk about. But let's not move too hastily. What I propose to do at this point is to pick up a central theme from my recent book *Sovereignty: God, State, and Self*,[1] and to refract our study of the humanities through its lens. Let's assume that I've already explored with you God's sovereignty and state sovereignty—I know that's a rather big assumption—and that we have now arrived at the sovereignty of selves, the notion that the self is self-sufficient, is a law unto itself, is the master of its own house. How did we get to be so, or to be seen as being so—this long story of the self alone, deserted on the little isle of the "I"?

This "I" is a creature of modernity, but is its triumph—the sovereign self—final? Is it complete? As I delved into this matter, I recognized—and it was only through hindsight that I did this, by going back over what I'd written—that the resources on which I drew to challenge the sovereign self, to salvage something deep and sustaining about an alternative view that I call the responsible self, came largely from the humanities, from the liberal arts more generally, from literature, from theological and ethical reflection.

Let me share with you the fruits of this labor, and perhaps we can together reflect on what it means to ask about the implications for education as the creation, the bringing into being, of selves of a certain kind. To repeat: if we look to liberal education to save us, then we are looking in the wrong place. But this doesn't mean that it cannot in vital ways illumine, sustain, and teach us.

With that, let me turn to words about the sovereign self and then offer powerful criticisms of this notion of the self.

The sovereign self is nothing if not prideful; this is a self that proclaims mastery, nigh total mastery. Might there not, however, be some irony here embedded, namely, that the notion of the sovereign self may in fact undermine the dignity of human persons? How is this so—how does this work? The answer lies in the fact that in making absolute human will and choice, we assault the relationality that alone lifts up and displays our humanity.

Albert Camus, one of the critics to whom I turn, is surely right, namely, that one who assumes absolute authority, in his words, lays "claim to nothing short of total freedom and the unlimited display of human pride. Nihilism confounds creator and created in the same blind fury. Suppressing every principle of hope, it rejects the idea of any limit. . . ."[2] For Camus, this is the dark night of nihilism and his reference is to twentieth-century totalitarian ideologies, but his words apply to any notion of total freedom, which implies, of course, the freedom to kill without limit in order to achieve one's ends.

Let me recast this in order to underscore certain salient points: personal autonomy, rightly understood, is a great achievement. Persons are not born as mature members of society, but they can grow to become such. Until they reach maturity, there are defensible reasons for treating them as immature beings in need of protection. Being a mature member of society does not entail complete independence from everybody else but, instead, requires a willingness and ability to build and to sustain rich relationships with other people. Given the historic achievements of self-sovereignty as well as its dangerous excesses—when man decides he is utterly autonomous, indeed godlike—we need other sorts of selves to forestall the worst. Contra Thomas Hobbes and Immanuel Kant, in their own distinctive ways, the subject is intrinsically relational.

Indeed, the person before me sets a limit to my own projects. The responsible self acknowledges the one before her and lives in the dialogic space thus created. Camus reminds us that the will to dominate and the will to submit are part and parcel of the same triumph of the will and certainly not the stuff out of which grows the responsible life. As well, the self cannot be what St. Augustine calls the proud "selfsame," a point of reference unto itself. In strong versions of sovereignty, the self shoulders on alone as the self is entirely volitional and grounds all reality, whether in the form of the self-maximizer of *homo economicus*, the biologically reductionist self of genetic engineering fantasies, or other candidates for contemporary sovereign selves.

By contrast, the self I have in mind seeks meaning and dignity and finds a measure of both not in total liberation from nature or total domination over nature or, alternatively, in some utopian attunement and oneness with nature, but rather in growing to become a person according to our human nature. Because that nature is intrinsically social, we must refrain from doing everything of which we are capable. If we refuse to observe a limit, we become destroyers. Camus describes the process of becoming a self as a much harder birth than one's first: " . . . to be born as a man and then to be born in a harder childbirth, which consists of being born in relation to others. . . ." These are words St. Augustine would understand, as he would appreciate Camus' insistence that we are born to and for joy and gratitude. In his posthumously published novel *The First Man*, the young boy Camus describes in this eloquent semi-autobiography "felt tears coming to his eyes along with a great cry of joy and gratitude for this wonderful life."[3]

Above all, we are created to love and to be loved. Think of the human beings we downgrade or who, in our benighted twentieth-century past, were targeted for destruction by National Socialism or communism, including persons with mental capacities who could not reason ("idiots and imbeciles and morons" in the gentle language of the time), all those who were infirm, dependent. What such selves have in common is that they cannot be sovereign in the manner extolled and assumed by self-sovereignty. They become a problem at present to and for liberal societies that presuppose that selves are freestanding and completely autonomous.

In our society at the moment, and in Western democracies in general, we are pursuing a paradoxical project: we are more aware of those with physical and mental disabilities; we want to provide them access. Yet at the same time, many of our most enthused-about projects aim at creating a world with no such persons in it. We will genetically engineer them away, and, until that time, we can eliminate them through selective abortion—the fate of around 87% of Down Syndrome pregnancies in the United States. And all of this occurs with no apparent regard for how persons with disabilities might, and indeed have, come to the conclusion that so-called "right to die" statutes are a way to say "right to eliminate non-sovereign selves" and that this just might threaten them. When we read that there have been at least 200 cases of euthanizing spina bifida infants in the Netherlands, it gives concrete evidence that such fears are not misplaced.

So where do we turn for alternatives?

I have suggested that we look at moral fables in order to fight contemporary *excarnation*—a term used by the philosopher Charles Taylor. Such fables warn us of hubristic overreach, of *superbia*, human pride; of run-amok *curiositas*, a curiosity turned deadly as it recognizes no limit, no constraint. Writes literary critic Roger Shattuck, concerning Mary Shelley, the author of the famous story of Dr. Frankenstein, "Her judgment of the presumptuous and selfish actions of Frankenstein in creating and then abandoning a new form of life" is instructive. "Apparently, it required a woman to inventory the destruction caused by the quest for knowledge and glory carried to excess, and to invent the counterplot to *Faust*."[4] Well, it doesn't really require a woman, as we find a similar motif and warning in the moral fable of Jekyll and Hyde by Robert Louis Stevenson.

The point is thus: we experiment with our natures at our peril. By "experiment with our natures," I do not, of course, mean "attempt to forestall terrible illness," say, or healing injury. The reductionistic argument often thrown in the face of one calling for limits is ridiculous; to wit, "I see, well, because it means messing with our natures, I guess you would never have wanted pneumonia to be treated or a polio vaccine developed." One sees how beside the point is such a rejoinder. By assisting us in being whole in body and spirit, as whole as we can be given what was given us at birth, we help to complete our natures, not to alter them radically. So we return to classic moral fables to instruct us on the excesses of sovereign selves.

One feature of celebrations of, and arguments for, self-sovereignty is a strange abstractedness, a refusal to keep one's feet on terra firma, perhaps because that reminds us of "from dust to dust," that we are earthy and earth-bound creatures. We can soar only if we are disembodied: the phenomenon Taylor calls modern excarnation. This invites a hyperexaggerated notion of what can be achieved through various philosophical modalities: we create systems, we live in our own heads, we expect selves and society to conform and then we shall have established sovereign control.

But if we lose our embodied, relational selves, which should make us less all-knowing, less harsh, we also lose dialogue, we lose a sense of what is appropriate to, and achievable by, creatures like ourselves. We also lose history—the living incarnational realities of human life in common. As Pope Benedict XVI argues, without embodied history, political theory becomes an entirely Gnostic enterprise—all words, no flesh; all spirit, no body.

Truly to fight excarnation requires that certain possibilities have not been smashed altogether. Here there is reason to be hopeful—not optimistic, but hopeful. Consider the horrific world limned by Primo Levi in his classic, *Survival in Auschwitz*. It is impossible to imagine a world more cruelly designed to defeat the human person than that demonic social experiment, the death camp. Levi alerts us, yet again, to the fact that the camps flowed directly from a process of reason, a terrible rationalism played out to the bitter end. Nazism was not a vast irrationalism at all. There is a major premise, a syllogism, and the end of the chain is the death camp. If indeed there are "lives unworthy of life," it follows inexorably that those who are "worthy of life"—sovereign selves—must remove those "unworthy of life" who have already been defined out of the human universe in any case.

Levi characterizes life in the camp as a "journey toward nothingness." But then he says something remarkable. "Yet no world of perfect unhappiness can exist. Our human condition is opposed to everything infinite. There is a limit on every joy and on every grief." In the camps, human beings were reduced to phantoms, their bodies disappearing. The demolition of man, Levi calls this. Your life was reduced to the lowest level. You were a "man who is no longer a man." First, Levi tells us, they annihilate you as a person, and then they kill you. It isn't enough just to kill you. They must kill the human spirit first, and our spirits are fragile. And yet . . . and yet . . . . The conviction that "life has a purpose is rooted in every fiber of man," and for some inmates of the camps surviving the "insane dream of grandeur of their masters" kept them going.[5]

Levi keeps his own sense of purpose alive by attempting to recall "The Canto of Ulysses" from Dante's *Divine Comedy*: there was beauty and form and sense in the world; there might be again. Levi concludes his haunting memoir, a moral fable of the twentieth century, the most horrible of all centuries, in this way: "No human experience is without meaning or unworthy of analysis." In the camps thousands of human beings who differed in "just about every way people can differ" were "thrown into a vast social experiment." And out of this he learns that human beings are not "fundamentally brutal at base." It is "far more complicated." Many social habits can be "silenced, quashed." But they *cannot be destroyed utterly.*⁶

If Primo Levi can redeem this much from the demonic horrors of the death camps, surely we can find resources on which to draw as we look to common sense, decency, dignity, to our sense of shame, our capacity for joy, our ability to recognize when our dignity is affronted, our ability to love, not just to use, others. The non-sovereign self has readier access to all of this precisely because he or she finds intimations and realizations of such a self all around, sees beauty, sadness, hope, mystery, truths to be found and discerned, as part of the very fabric of the universe.

Several other writers come to mind to help us combat modern excarnality, to tame self-sovereignty. The great poet Czeslaw Milosz and the novelist Marilynne Robinson understand that persons, by contrast to isolated individuals, are unique and unrepeatable. They cannot simply be replaced by a new recruit. Each understands that pure thought is not greater than love. The Nobel laureate Milosz is also the author of one of the great books assaying the nature of the totalitarian, *The Captive Mind.* This great work was derided by man when it was first published in the early 1950s, attacked by those still enamored of the world-historical project of Marxism. Indeed, Milosz told me over the course of a dinner conversation that he had been informed by a member of his tenure review committee at the University of California, Berkeley, that he received tenure in spite of the fact that he had written such a politically incorrect book.

If we take a look at *The Captive Mind*, we enter a world of incarnationality and leave behind a world of lifeless ratiocination. Here I have in mind Milosz's determination to be fleshly, concrete, and particular. An incarnational text is a world of concrete presences: it derives from an impulse to make real that which is symbolized or represented. A symbol, a metaphor, a figure does not stand apart from but participates in "the thing itself," so to speak. The writer aims neither for a pure realm nor an ideal form but for a way to express reverence for that which simply *is*, most importantly the flesh and blood human beings around us.

I think, for example, of my favorite passage from *The Captive Mind*, in which Milosz describes walking through a train station in Ukraine in the desperately disordered time of the beginning of World War II. He is caught up short by the following scene:

> A peasant family—husband and wife and two children—had settled down by the wall. They were sitting on baskets and bundles. The wife was feeding the younger child; the husband who had a dark, wrinkled face and a black, drooping mustache was pouring tea out of a kettle into a cup for the older boy. They were whispering to each other in Polish. I gazed at them until I felt moved to the point of tears. What had stopped my steps so suddenly and touched me so profoundly was their *difference*. This was a human group, an island in a crowd that lacked something proper to humble, ordinary human life. The gesture of a hand pouring tea, the careful, delicate handing of the cup to the child, the worried words I guessed from the movement of their lips, their isolation, their privacy in the midst of the crowd—that is what moved me. For a moment, then, I understood something that quickly slipped from my grasp.[7]

Perhaps, one might suggest, there is something about the fragility and miracle of the quotidian. Milosz is rightly celebrated for capturing such moments in his poetry, moments that quickly slip or threaten to slip from our grasp. His poems, he tells us, are encounters with the peculiar circumstances of time and space. The portrait of that forlorn bit of humanity, huddled together, uprooted, yet making and pouring tea—this says something about the quotidian. For Milosz, the touchstone for twentieth-century politics was terror and the immediacy of stark, physical pain—a phenomenon that self-encloses us, cuts us off. And yet... those cries can still be heard if our thinking is not excarnated and remote. We can still acknowledge the delicate ritual of the family making tea.

The twentieth-century mind was susceptible to seduction by socio-political doctrines that abstractly dealt out death. The twenty-first century has already treated us to examples of the same. Milosz puts on display the impoverished, one-dimensional, flattened-out view of human beings that a totalizing ideology of politics and self-sovereignty requires and feeds on. He indicts the "vulgarized" knowledge that gives birth to the feeling that everything is controllable, for example, "the young cannibals who, in the name of inflexible principles, butchered the population of Cambodia" and "who had graduated from the Sorbonne and were simply trying to implement the philosophic ideas they had learned."

In her award-winning novel *Gilead*, the novelist Marilynne Robinson opens up a world of simple and complex beauties and often unremarked goodness. "Any human face is a claim on you," her protagonist, the dying pastor, John Ames, writes, "because you can't help but understand the singularity of it, the courage and loneliness of it." In her incarnational writing, she highlights the "body blessed and broken" in Christian theology and in everyday life. Pastor Ames talks about the gift of "physical particularity and how blessing and sacrament are mediated through it."[8] It follows that God's love and mortal love are not so separate. There is a splendor "revealed" in a child's face. Robinson's protagonist also reminds us that the great Hebrew prophets of Scripture chastised and loved a concrete people, something too many moderns who don the mantle of prophecy seem to have abandoned as they despise those they criticize and the country that is their home.

We also have theologians to whom we can turn, those who insist on the concrete living realities of communities and the relational dimensions of all human propensities and projects. What theologian Alistair McFadyen in *Bound to Sin* alerts us to is the harm—the "deeply distorting, distorted and damaging relationship"—that results when some human beings are systematically harmed by others, calling this recognition a "relational ecology." This reminds us that every human being enters the world under a burden of history and that history teaches us—or should—to beware "highly optimistic assessment of the possibilities of reason."[9] Even the architects of Nazi genocide found it difficult to kill face to face, or to witness such killing, or to view the aftermath of it. In implementing their plans for mass murder, they required a distance that eliminated the moral space of the "in-between" myself and another.

Narrow rationalism tethered to boundless will generated a tyrannical nightmare. The upshot for McFadyen? We must reject certain dichotomies: it is neither autonomy, nor abject surrender. God is neither utterly transcendent—so removed there is no coherent analogy relating God to our selves—nor so entirely immanent that we are simply subsumed into this god-substance and become indistinguishable from it. This ecology of relationship does not treat human beings as agglomerates delimited by race or sex or class or some other category made absolute; no, the dignity of the human person is irreducible and cannot be wholly subsumed into these abstract categories.

Anti-Nazi theologian Dietrich Bonhoeffer reminds us throughout his work that "bodilyness and human life belong inseparably together" and this has "very far-reaching consequences" for our understanding of every aspect of human life, for we can use our bodies and those of others well or ill."[10] The right to live is, for Bonhoeffer, of the "very essence"; indeed, even the most "wretched life" is "worth living before God." What should continuously amaze us is that many of the lives we imagine to be utterly wretched are, in fact, not: people find purpose and even joy in the midst of extraordinary difficulty and suffering. This is not all they find, of course, but we can see redemptive moments where we might least expect them.

> Freedom is not a quality of man, nor is it an ability . . . it is not a possession, a presence, an object, nor is it a form of existence—but a relationship and nothing else. In truth, freedom is a relationship between two persons. Being free means "being free for the other," because the other has bound me to him. In relationship with the other I am free.[11]

These are strong words that bespeak incarnational realities. Human life is always lived in concrete communities, not in nowhere. Even as God is dialogic and related and giving of himself, so are we called to be likewise. In a society such as ours, with our history, these recognitions can be continuously rekindled and no doubt resources from other faiths offer similar possibilities of renewal. Oversimply, we are never in a zero-sum game in this life of ours, never in a situation in which the exact sum I "give" is something taken away from me absolutely and appropriated by someone else: that is Sartre's "hell is other people," a desolate, dead, and lonely world. It is not the world of people who embrace the quotidian rather than despise it, who find joy in simple things, who find dignity in a decent job well done. Our bodies define a limit, yes, but also a possibility as we enter into community, for we can "be" by virtue of others.

Augustine's fear was that as we gave up on God's sovereignty, then other forms of human sovereignty, not of the chastened or limited sort, would drive to become superordinate and destructive in the ways I have assayed. Augustine was keenly aware of the fact that any human institution can be turned into an idolatry, whether of family or state, or anything else. The altar at which we worship nowadays is the sovereign self whose key terms are control, doing your own thing, choice as a kind of willfulness rather than as the sometimes tragic weighing of options when there is no hands-down good or bad on either side. The Augustinian pilgrim is one who can challenge the idolatries of his or her age without opting out, as if one could, or fleeing into a realm at least theoretically removed from the vortex of social and political life

I turn now to some concluding thoughts from Albert Camus, a thinker who lived through and was defined by the culture of self-criticism so characteristic of the West. He was an unbeliever, not an atheist, he said, one who lived in an ongoing dialogue with Christians. He understood our indebtedness to those who had gone before, who had crafted the possibilities for such a culture, for Europe at her best. Exploring a world of moral relativism and absolute nihilism, Camus indicts philosophies that are used as goads or alibis for abstract mass murder, indicts those who take refuge in ideologies and erect slave camps under the flag of freedom. In his great essay *The Rebel*, he writes,

> If we believe in nothing, if nothing has any meaning and we can affirm no values whatsoever, then everything is possible and nothing has any importance. There is no pro or con: the murderer is neither right nor wrong. We are free to stoke the crematory fires or to devote ourselves to the care of lepers.... Since nothing is either true or false, good or bad, our guiding principle will be to demonstrate that we are the most efficient, in other words, the strongest. That is the only measure of success.[12]

Camus here sketches a world of the will-to-power triumphant, a world of "executioners and victims," as he put it. And how does one tell the story of this triumph? It is nothing less than "the history of European pride." In rebelling against a world that is cruel or murderous or systematically unjust, the authentic rebel observes a limit. He affirms the "existence of a borderline ... that there are limits and also that he respects—and wishes to preserve—the existence of certain things on this side of the borderline." When a person rebels, he identifies himself with others, according to Camus, rather than repudiating them utterly. He eschews resentment, a corrosive envy of what one does not have. The authentic rebel wishes to defend what he in fact is: a human being, a person. And in rebellion he finds not isolation, but solidarity. So strong is Camus' claim in this regard that he declares that anyone who "claims the right" to destroy this "solidarity loses [the] right to be called rebellion and becomes instead acquiescent in murder." For rebellion "must respect the limit it discovers in itself—a limit where minds meet and, in meeting, begin to exist. I rebel, therefore we exist."[13]

The alternative is unlimited freedom, the "negation of others and the suppression of pity." What is a totalitarian society but a story of unbridled freedom to kill? The nihilist would become godlike, a rival of the Creator, perpetually demanding some sort of unity (of victim and victimizer) with hatred of the creator transmogrified into hatred of creation. Augustine and Camus would come together in an answer to what happens to people who live without grace and without justice. Nihilism supplies the answer. A frenzied will to power triumphs. Finally, one must insist, Camus tells us, on the fact that there is a human nature and resist all attempts to turn it into the rubble of historic forces.

> Absolute revolution presupposes the absolute malleability of human nature and its possible reduction to the condition of a historical force. But rebellion, in man, is the refusal to be treated as an object and to be reduced to simple historical terms. It is the affirmation of a nature common to all men, which eludes the world of power.[14]

These are words at which the totalitarian would scoff and which the radical postmodern could never speak. But speak such words we must, and Camus reminds us that the fruit of Western culture requires that we remember both Jerusalem and Athens, belief and unbelief, faith and skepticism. And, for Camus, the beauty of this world, and our ability to respond to it, is one possible source for regeneration of our culture, which recalls "the common dignity of man and the world he lives in and which we must now define in the face of a world that insults it."[15]

In Camus' novel *The Plague*, the narrator, Dr. Rieux, "bears witness" to the sufferings of innocent people laid low by the terror of the plague. After the plague is gone and people greet one another in open plazas and laugh and drink and eat, Rieux warns that we should never be complacent, never smug:

> Nonetheless, he [Rieux] knew that the tale he had to tell could not be one of final victory. It could be only the record of what had had to be done, and what assuredly would have to be done again in the never ending fight against terror and its relentless onslaughts, despite their personal afflictions, by all who, unable to be saints but refusing to bown down to pestilences, strive their utmost to be healers.
>
> And, indeed, as he listened to the cries of joy rising from the town, Rieux remembered that such joy is always imperiled. He knew what those jubilant crowds did not know but could have learned from books: that the plague bacillus never dies or disappears for good; that it can lie dormant for years and years in furniture and linen-chests; that it bides its time in bedrooms, cellars, trunks, and bookshelves; and that perhaps the day would come when, for the bane and the enlightening of men, it would rouse up its rats again and send them forth to die in a happy city.[16]

Selves that are less-than-sovereign understand this moral allegory and live with this mordant recognition. Far easier to be comfortably sovereign and "in control." But then one lives in a kind of dreamworld that will fade or crash to bits as all dreams of incandescent glory can and must. Selves immersed in a world with and among their fellow human beings, that relational ecology we have noted, affirm, respect, and find joy in life's everydayness and its simple joys and pleasures.

3

SCHOLARSHIP IN ACTION AND THE PUBLIC MISSION OF UNIVERSITIES

— *Nancy Cantor* —

Chancellor and President, Syracuse University

At key points in our nation's history, we've turned to our colleges and universities to serve as engines for prosperity and agents of social mobility. This is such a moment. Times are hard, and we are called to help revive our economy and sustain our communities while opening our doors even wider to a whole generation of talented youth: the fast-growing population of students who will be the first in their families to go to college, the sons and daughters of newly immigrated families, veterans returning from post-9/11 conflicts, and the students who are now in often under-resourced inner-city and rural schools. We must find ways to welcome them to our ranks.

The challenge, as I would frame it, is to engage our students and faculty and staff in creative work that is tuned to the world's most pressing issues as we as institutions become more innovative, effective, and valuable, as we become vital contributors to a newly thriving America. At the same time—to draw on the wise words of our neighbors in Syracuse, the Onondaga Nation—we must be ever vigilant for the well-being of the "seventh generation yet to come."

History shows that higher education can do this. Nearly 150 years ago, between the years in which Baylor and Syracuse were founded, when the Civil War threatened the very existence of our nation, we were challenged to tap the productivity of our land and the promise of the Industrial Age. President Lincoln had the foresight to see beyond the conflict and sign into law the Morrill Act—the landmark legislation creating our land-grant university system to conserve, encourage, and promote agriculture, which employed more than half the nation's population and deeply influenced its prosperity.[1]

Today, in many respects, we are again in such an era. This time, we are making a transition from an industrial to a knowledge economy. Once again, our nation and our world are challenged by conflict and divisions. In our so-called flat, fully wired, and interconnected world—where nearly 70% of Americans live in metropolitan areas—there are thousands who are not connected at all, who are falling further and further behind in education, income, and employment.[2] Simultaneously, the aftereffects of industry and overconsumption have given warning that our natural resources are fast becoming depleted. The sustainability of our water, energy, food, and land—resources all absolutely critical for our survival on this planet—unfortunately has also become an issue that has pitted whole groups, cultures, and religions against one another, as if we've forgotten how to raise a barn together!

Against this fraught backdrop—and with an eye on that seventh generation yet to come—it is imperative that great institutions roll up their sleeves and get to the world's work. If not, we should rightly be criticized for breaking our social compact, whether we are public or private, religiously affiliated or not. As your new President, Ken Starr, wrote recently in the journal *First Things*, "All too often, the modern academy appears as something smugly remote and arrogantly aloof from the people who support and sustain it."[3] We cannot afford, nor should we want, to be tarred with that description. And in very deep ways, it would be inconsistent with the legacies of commitment to public engagement at both of our institutions.

In the case of Syracuse, for example, World War II was a defining moment for our institutional identity. Overnight, we literally tripled our enrollment to welcome returning veterans on the GI Bill. Today we still proudly embrace our veterans and support their road to opportunity, breaking new ground with our award-winning Entrepreneurs Bootcamp for Veterans with Disabilities that has expanded to include five other universities, from Connecticut to California.

Baylor's touchstone is ensconced in your motto—"*Pro Ecclesia*" followed by "*Pro Texana.*" Your passionate embrace of faith serves as a motivator for public service, a tradition with roots in your very founding. It is a living legacy, as expressed by the desires of "nearly one-third of first-year Baylor students to pursue careers in health care," as President Starr proudly described in his essay "The Soul of a College."

Syracuse and Baylor are both private research universities that are acutely aware of their responsibility to serve the public good. A modern research university can and should go beyond its boundaries to tackle the "messy" intractable problems that are best addressed through many disciplines with many partners, on campus and off. Education, side by side with research embedded in our rich array of academic disciplines, can make a huge impact in partnerships of all kinds with our many communities.

The Third Spaces of Public Engagement

In Syracuse, where the city's population has been moving to the suburbs for the last fifty years, Syracuse University (SU) is a critical anchor institution in turning our community around. We see quite directly how important the public mission of higher education can be to a prosperous future. We are deeply engaged with local issues that resonate globally, from environmental sustainability to urban education, working with many partners and creating "third spaces" of interaction built around major projects that engage faculty and students by intertwining learning, scholarship, and civic engagement. We call this vision Scholarship in Action.

One such "third space" is our city's Near Westside, with its iconic centerpiece, St. Lucy's Church, where Father Jim Mathews proudly "welcomes all, sinners and saints alike," to this beleaguered but deeply soulful neighborhood. This was once a thriving district of factories, railyards, and housing where people could walk to work—one factory had more than two thousand employees and not one place to park! It was one of the neighborhoods hardest hit during the city's industrial decline. The Near Westside now includes the second poorest cluster of census tracts in the nation. It is a multiethnic and multiracial community with enormous human potential, despite the profound challenges that arise from the deep chasms that divide our society and our world. On the Near Westside, 50% of the 3,300 residents live below the poverty line, 40% are unemployed, and 37% consider themselves to have one or more disabilities.

Over the years, as housing vacancies went up and property values went down, the dilapidated properties in this neighborhood were snapped up by slumlords who collected the rents but rarely made repairs. Many of them live out of town, where they don't have to see the landscape they have made: 152 vacant parcels of land and 83 vacant structures in an area of less than a third of a square mile.

Several years ago, SU joined with foundations, businesses, not-for-profits, state and city governments, and, most importantly, neighborhood residents: from grandmothers with the wisdom of the ages to the deeply committed priest of St. Lucy's to the youth who will ultimately save this neighborhood. Together they created a nonprofit organization, the Near Westside Initiative, as an exciting and (we hope) deeply democratic partnership that embeds the arts, technology, and design with other fields—architecture, entrepreneurship, law, education, environmental engineering, public health, and public communications, to name a few—as catalysts for change.

The Near Westside Initiative seeks not to gentrify the neighborhood—which ultimately merely sweeps problems under the rug—but to transform the neighborhood from the inside out with the community's residents at the table. And we have multiple nonprofit partners who have long worked with residents to address housing issues piece by piece. Their collective action, connected to the efforts of many others, is producing results that have truly transformative potential.

Home HeadQuarters, a not-for-profit organization, has acquired 103 residential parcels within the target area and to date has rehabilitated thirteen properties, constructed seven new green residences on vacant properties, and marketed and sold five vacant, dilapidated properties for one dollar each to new homeowners. Christopher Community has built sixty new affordable rental properties, and Habitat for Humanity has constructed nine new homes since the Initiative began.

For our part, SU is leveraging some longstanding strengths to make residential and commercial buildings in the neighborhood more sustainable. For example, our School of Architecture teamed up with our green technologists to conduct an international competition to create cutting-edge, green, single-family homes designed specifically for sites on the Near Westside. Three of the winning designs are under construction and are near completion. Even in our frigid, snowy winters, one of these homes is so well insulated it can be heated with the energy it would take to run a hair dryer!

All told, since the inception of the Near Westside Initiative, the neighborhood has seen more than $12 million in residential property acquisition, rehabilitation, and new construction, providing families with housing options that are safe and affordable—and energy efficient, which is no small thing in our climate!

These efforts have stimulated very encouraging economic activity. Two of the warehouses being redeveloped are drawing artists and arts-based businesses and nonprofits to the neighborhood, including ProLiteracy, the world's largest literacy organization, with 135 employees, and our regional public television affiliate, WCNY, with 80 employees. New York State's oldest architectural firm, a bookstore, a recording studio, a coffee shop, a fitness center, and a bakery have all been attracted to the neighborhood over the past two years.

To create wealth that is rooted in the neighborhood, two resident-owned cooperatives are being launched: a high-tech hydroponic greenhouse that will grow and sell fresh vegetables, and a "Green Property Management Company" to maintain nearly 300,000 square feet of mixed-use properties owned and operated by the Near Westside Initiative. These properties are both commercial and residential, and the new co-op will use environmentally sound practices and products to keep them up.

At this point, you might well say, "That's great for the city, the neighborhood, and the residents, but it sounds a lot like the traditional economic development that universities have long sought for their communities. What does it do for higher education at the university?"

Well, the answer is, "a lot."

"Third spaces" like the Near Westside give our faculty and our students unparalleled opportunities for cutting edge research and for creativity that really matters. Scholarship in Action is, in fact, a two-way street of engagement that traverses our campus and community.

Collaborative "Laboratories" for Scholarship in Action

To give you one example, the green technologists involved in the neighborhood are from the Syracuse Center of Excellence in Environmental and Energy Systems. SU hosts this Center, but its assets are distributed among twelve core universities and research institutes, industry partners across our region, and government agencies at all levels. All of them have a "second home" (and for some a "first home") in the new state-of-the-art facility recently erected for the Center on a remediated brownfield site in downtown Syracuse. Many years ago, it was the site of the Smith Typewriter Company—before it became Smith Corona, producing the typewriters that were a staple of every business office until computers made them obsolete.

The regional, federation approach to environmental issues that the Center of Excellence is taking allows us to assemble entrepreneurial, agile, cross-sector, crossdisciplinary teams to take on sustainability problems wherever they arise. We find ourselves breaking down academic and organizational silos both through necessity and the interests of our partners, because solving complex environmental problems demands this kind of broad collaboration. Crucially, this opens up the process for setting the research agenda and for integrating the perspectives and interests of public, private, and nonprofit partners.

In partnership with the Near Westside Initiative, the Center of Excellence has an extraordinary real-world test bed for energy-efficient building innovations at every stage: from research and development to demonstration, commercialization, and deployment. For example, we've conducted a federally funded study that documents the impact of poor housing conditions locally on childhood asthma incidence. We've also funded research that has resulted in the development of air purification systems that dramatically reduce childhood asthma.

The Center worked with US GreenBuild to prototype what a whole neighborhood LEED certification system could look like, including a green retrofit plan for housing. It also is working in a partnership with the EPA, the local utility National Grid, and Home HeadQuarters to conduct free energy audits of existing businesses and homes. The goal is to identify affordable energy-efficiency upgrades for commercial and residential buildings and then to help owners apply for the financing to get them done.

We've also overseen the complete, green renovation of a four-story warehouse that includes a geothermal field, solar panels, hot water on demand, and an innovative living wall screen over part of the building, as well as rainwater recycling capacity.

In fact, we're now leading an effort to scale up the impact of this kind of cross-sector collaboration across New York State, drawing in numerous other partners connected all along the "value chain" of energy-efficient building systems. We intend to form a massive New York Energy Regional Innovation Cluster that can unite the R&D and manufacturing capacities located in Upstate New York with one of the world's largest real estate markets, Downstate New York, including New York City.

So you can see why our scientists, engineers, architects, designers, real estate economists, and public policy experts are excited about the incredibly fertile ground for research—the "collaborative laboratory"—that we're cultivating. And it has all started right in our neighborhood with our many partners, where our faculty can see that the work they're doing locally in Syracuse resonates powerfully both within their academic fields and across communities around the world.

EDUCATION FOR THE WORLD, IN THE WORLD

At research universities like Baylor and Syracuse, where we have worked hard to integrate excellent research with superb teaching, we know we must seize every opportunity to bring students into our laboratories on campus. Likewise, it is absolutely essential to realize that the laboratories we have created with our community partners also constitute optimal learning environments for our students, where they can prepare *for* the world, *in* the world.

As you might imagine, the opportunities for teaching, learning, and research that we find in community contexts like the Near Westside extend across the full range of disciplines and take many forms. Professor Marion Wilson, a sculptor who is director of community initiatives in our School of Education, has been using the Near

Westside as a studio for what she calls "social sculpture," named after the concept put forward by Josef Beuys, that sculpture is not only object making but can also be thought, experience, and how we mold and shape the world.

With a crossdisciplinary team of faculty and students from the arts, humanities, education, ecology, and business management, Professor Wilson is spearheading a project to transform a former drug house across the street from an elementary school from a menace to a promise. The two-story house was stripped down to its studs and is being reimagined and rebuilt with recycled materials by an academically diverse team over a period of three semesters, an effort that requires both community support and planning permission from city officials.

As Professor Wilson told the zoning officials, the work at 601 Tully Street will "make it less of an object than a living thing that changes the way we live." That change started with the zoning meeting itself, which was jammed by so many students, faculty members, and community partners, including a high school student who gave a long and impassioned speech in favor of the project, that the chair was moved to remark, "We're not used to having this big a crowd. We hope you enjoy yourselves."

The structure at 601 Tully will feature a center for arts education, a place where faculty member and photographer Steve Mahan, can teach both SU students and high school students together in his pioneering course on photography and literacy. As he says, "We're going in and using photography as a storytelling device . . . You can tell a story without being able to read on a certain level or write on a certain level. English doesn't have to be your first language. You might have Asperger's, autism, a learning disability, whatever you want to call it. Instantly, right off the bat, the camera seems to level that playing field."

For Syracuse University students, courses like these taught in community and with students from the city schools become an eye-opening opportunity to be both expert and novice, teacher and learner, all in one experience, as they and their school district "peers" each find their vision and voice. The plan is for 601 Tully to house a coffee shop and bookstore run by students from the business academy at nearby Fowler High School, so this piece of social sculpture will also become a place to cultivate entrepreneurs.

In a parallel project, one of our communications design classes spent the entire spring semester last year creating designs—from banners on the street to maps for visitors—to help the community visually mark the identity of the Near Westside neighborhood closest to the school and to downtown as the SALT District, the Syracuse Art, Literacy, and Technology District.

Our students, many of them from the suburbs, became fascinated by the large number of ugly fences they saw here, some of them enclosing large empty lots for no obvious purpose. "What does a fence mean?" they asked each other. "Would it be possible to make fences like these beautiful rather than intimidating?"

They researched and proposed a number of designs, and last summer one of the students, Stephanie Hart, a junior from Keene, New Hampshire, spent the whole summer working on it as an intern without pay. She consulted with community groups on the design and then worked with local children and youth to snap six thousand colored pieces of plastic into eleven sections of the six foot Anchor fence around Skiddy Park, the playground on the side of Tully Street across from the elementary school.

Each day, she walked over to the park from downtown with a cart, carrying fifty pound boxes of diamond-shaped plastic inserts small enough to snap into the openings in the fence. As the design progressed—some of it changed by the kids who wanted to add things like flowers—a few passersby told Stephanie they thought the pieces would be popped out again before morning, but residents of the community liked it, and over the months, the design on the fence has survived.

"I'm definitely more comfortable in the neighborhood," Stephanie said as the work went on. "I have a lot more connections than I did before the summer started. I have an idea of what it takes to do community work: how many people you have to talk to before you get things approved, how much money things cost, and how much money we *don't* have to do those things."

Growing Entrepreneurship from the Ground Up

And speaking of resources, these experiences on the Near Westside translate into critical lessons about entrepreneurship—for students, faculty, and neighborhood residents alike. Seemingly simple interactions can spark insights into what it takes to grow entrepreneurship in our city and in others, like us, who are remaking themselves to compete in what Bruce Katz, head of The Brookings Institution's Metropolitan Policy Program, refers to as "The Next Economy"—one in which America must become low carbon and, once again, innovation driven and export oriented. If we are going to thrive in that economy, we need to grow a lot more entrepreneurs in our metropolitan areas.

As part of this effort, we've created a business incubator in the center of Syracuse's long-underserved South Side. Our South Side Innovation Center provides office space and business support for start up businesses and budding entrepreneurs, sharing common costs and equipment to reduce the expenses incurred in starting new businesses.

We're helping entrepreneurs forge links with one another—through the recently incorporated South Side Entrepreneurs Association, for example. We're connecting them with resources for their businesses: investors, talent, customers, and markets. We're also introducing them to the nonprofits, public sector organizations, and social service agencies geared toward building an entrepreneurial culture. SU has put its intellectual capital on the table through faculty-run educational programs and student consulting teams that help entrepreneurs who are already up and running hone their business plans.

We're starting to see incredibly promising results. In just three years, the Innovation Center has touched thousands of people through conferences and training programs. It has launched 77 new businesses and helped more than 550 existing businesses better tune their operations to their markets. It has created 72 local jobs and retained another 133.

One of the latest success stories is that of the East Environmental Group, LLC, a local, minority-owned business founded by Shawan East. They specialize in the abatement of hazardous air and building materials. From one employee, they've already grown to five, bought two other companies, and opened a second office in Binghamton, another city in Upstate New York.

Another new company, Bluetree Studios, owned by local resident Christiana Kaiser, specializes in West African imports and foods that are now stocked by fifty stores. She too has now opened up a second office.

The South Side Innovation Center also includes a Community Test Kitchen to help local food entrepreneurs. One of these, Stacey VanWaldick, hit the road to stardom with her business Promise Me Chocolate, which makes edible gems from chocolate. Her chocolates made Oprah's "O List" for the 2009 holiday season and were featured by *Martha Stewart Weddings* magazine.

We're also taking these successes in the community back to campus along the two-way street of Scholarship in Action because we know we have a lot to learn about cultivating our own entrepreneurs—and with an entrepreneurship program as strong as you have here at Baylor, you know exactly what I mean.

We're doing this through a university-wide program to infuse the entrepreneurial spirit across the curriculum—and this is entrepreneurship writ large. Extending beyond traditional notions of honing one's business acumen, we are empowering faculty, students, and professionals of all stripes to activate their intellectual capital, share it generously with others, collaborate with communities of experts, and make a difference in the world by launching new ventures specifically in our city and region.

This "E-nitiative," as we call it, is leveraged by a five-year, $3 million grant from the Kauffman Foundation to pool expertise across six public and private institutions, businesses, and nonprofits in Central New York. The goal is to use the experience of successful venture capitalists and entrepreneurs to mentor the next generation.

So far the results are promising. Over the first three years, we've supported more than 150 projects. We've more than tripled enrollment in entrepreneurship courses across our partner institutions—from 1,900 to 6,600. And our "Student Sandbox" business incubator is bursting at the seams with fifteen student startups in residence right now.

One of these startups is called *brand-yourself.com*. It empowers subscribers to manage the many, sometimes unwieldy aspects of their online presence—a tool we found so practical for newly minted college graduates that we gave subscriptions as a graduation gift to our entire class of 2010. We feel it will be invaluable as they enter a job market where the virtual and physical worlds increasingly intersect.

Building Social Capital

Our expansive vision of entrepreneurship encompasses more than the business community. The idea is to reinforce and help sustain the tremendous *social* capital in the community through entrepreneurship. You can already see the progress on the South Side. As we were building the physical infrastructure for economic entrepreneurship, we were facilitating the emergence of an independent, community-based organization of neighborhood leaders.

We asked this group, the South Side Community Coalition, to identify and prioritize projects they consider essential to turning the neighborhood around. We also asked them to suggest a social infrastructure that can sustain economic development and community-wide revitalization. The Coalition compiled a formal Request for Proposals to the Syracuse University faculty to take on their highest priority projects. We, in turn, identified faculty members and students with the right expertise to partner with community members in these efforts.

As a result, the variety of projects now under way speaks both to the Coalition's thoughtful and visionary leadership and to the breadth of interest among SU's faculty to share what they know with—and to learn from—the local community.

For example, access to affordable, fresh produce has long has been an issue in this neighborhood that major chain grocery stores have utterly avoided. Our own scholarship over the years has shown that poor nutrition—the result of buying food from small corner stores that stock mostly liquor and lottery tickets, not fresh vegetables or fruit—has been a key factor in high rates of infant mortality.[4]

The South Side Community Coalition and Syracuse faculty have now collaborated to sponsor a farmers' market held seasonally in a centrally located parking lot in the heart of the South Side. Plans are in place for a permanent home for a locally owned food co-op.

We have been involved in health initiatives in this community for several years through the award-winning Genesis Health Project Network, a community-designed and culturally sensitive collaboration with the pastors and congregations of ten inner-city Black churches with more than three thousand members. Working with lay health advocates and local medical institutions, the Genesis Network meets residents where they live—for example, at barbershops and in churches—and provides education to reduce health disparities and obesity and to promote a healthy lifestyle among African Americans in low income areas of the city.[5]

Preserving the histories of families and social institutions also was identified as a key concern by neighborhood residents, so we've assembled a team of SU faculty and students spanning library science, museum studies, and communication and rhetorical studies to train residents to preserve cultural artifacts.

Together, they created a documentary film about the history of the neighborhood, which was and is predominantly African American, and we established a mechanism for training future generations to preserve their past—our present—creating a certificate program in the preservation of cultural heritage.

And, as we know, the news coming out of historically disempowered neighborhoods like the South Side is too often told from the perspective of people on the outside. So we're empowering the insiders—the residents—to report *their* news from *their* perspective, as faculty and students from our Newhouse School of Public Communications have partnered with residents to create a print and online community newspaper called *The Stand*.

EDUCATING OUR CHILDREN

Speaking of the news, as we're all aware, the state of urban schools has not been encouraging. Nationally, we see growing gaps in educational attainment between the public schools in our cities and our suburbs. High school students from low-income families are dropping out of school at six times the rate of high-income peers. The math achievement of African- and Latino- American seventeen-year-olds is trailing that of white students, and many bright but poor children are not receiving the encouragement and advice they need to pursue college.[6]

We have seen these trends play out locally in Syracuse, where 71% of Syracuse City School District students are from minority groups,[7] 75% receive free or reduced-price lunches, and less than 50% of the students entering kindergarten graduate high school thirteen years later.

Knowing that the hope of our city—indeed, the hope of cities like Syracuse all over America—rests on our ability to alter dramatically this picture, SU and the Syracuse City School District have undertaken a precedent-setting project in partnership with the Say Yes to Education Foundation. Together, we aim to alter the life course of students throughout our city by dramatically increasing the rate at which they attend college.

Building on the Foundation's track record of remarkable success in several urban schools in Harlem, Philadelphia, Hartford, Connecticut, and Cambridge, Massachusetts, we are scaling up the Say Yes model for the first time to the level of an entire district.

We emphasize that the persistent and well-documented "achievement gap" between urban students and their suburban peers is *not* an accurate measure of ability or potential but is actually an "opportunity" gap. Too many urban students have not had the *opportunity* to take full advantage of the academic and social supports that their more privileged peers have, experiences that lead to success in higher education. This gap shows up not only in grades but also in standardized-test scores, course selection, dropout rates, access to curriculum, and quality instruction. We see the results in high school graduation rates, and the differentials in college admission and college-completion rates.

Say Yes to Education: Syracuse closes the opportunity gap by providing crucial, comprehensive support to city's 21,000 public school students and their families. We are addressing many of the academic, health, social, emotional, and legal issues that so often act as insurmountable roadblocks to inner-city youth on the path to college.

Perhaps most importantly, the program helps students to overcome one of the biggest barriers of all: the cost of higher education.

Through the Say Yes Higher Education Compact, Syracuse City School District students have access to tuition scholarship support at two dozen private institutions and SUNY/CUNY—and we have sent about one thousand students to college through Say Yes in the last two years.

To date, we have rolled out our comprehensive program in three of the city's four quadrants, with after-school programs at eighteen schools and an academically oriented summer camp attended by 1,600 students this past summer. We have dramatically reduced caseloads for school social workers. Five private law firms and five nonprofits are providing free legal assistance to district families, and we're piloting a health insurance program for them.

Because we know that the prosperity of our city is at stake, we're very encouraged by the early indicators of the sweeping impact of Say Yes. We've seen enrollment in the city schools increase for the first time in a decade—by three hundred this fall—which tells us that parents are choosing to move to or keep their children in city schools. We've seen median home sales values increase by 3.5%, even with a persistently sluggish real estate market. And we've already seen the dropout rate for ninth grade fall over the past two years. These early signs of progress are, we believe, a bellweather of the more transformative influence yet to come, as all of the educational and family supports take root and the community begins really to believe that all of our City children can thrive on a path toward postsecondary education.

Transformative Impact for Universities and Communities

Transformation. This is our aim for Say Yes and, in fact, for all the projects we're undertaking under the banner of Scholarship in Action. We are looking to transform the world and, because this is a two-way street, we are looking to transform ourselves. Scholarship in Action has enriched our thinking about our students and how they learn. It has inspired and excited members of our faculty who have found expansive opportunities for research and creativity while creating optimal learning environments. It has expanded our criteria for rewarding excellence among our faculty as we embed structures for public scholarship in our tenure and promotion guidelines. And it has profoundly changed our relationship with the world through reciprocal partnerships that bring us to the world and the world to us.

The work is not easy. When we are challenged to see through the eyes of others, as we are so frequently and poignantly by children, we often are forced to confront inequities that we didn't see before.

But we should not be surprised that the work is not easy, and we, like the Baylor community, are ready to roll up our institutional sleeves and try to make a difference in our world. For though Syracuse's institutional history and geography may lie on a different path than Baylor's, I suspect that when we face these challenges, we sometimes find inspiration in the same places. I know that I often find it in the words of a famous Baptist, the Reverend Dr. Martin Luther King Jr., who eloquently described the dissatisfaction with the status quo—for King, it was "divine dissatisfaction"—that in some important ways captures the underlying motivation that led so many of us in academe to the path we are on.

As we think today about the challenges we face in transforming our academic communities and working for justice and prosperity in the communities where we are situated, as well as in our nation and our world, Dr. King's rallying cry rings out as loud and clear as it did more than forty years ago, when he said,

> "Let us be dissatisfied until America will no longer have a high blood pressure of creeds and an anemia of deeds...
>
> "Let us be dissatisfied until the tragic walls that separate the outer city of wealth and comfort from the inner city of poverty and despair shall be crushed by the battering rams of the forces of justice...
>
> "Let us be dissatisfied until slums are cast into the junk heaps of history and every family will live in a decent, sanitary home.
>
> "Let us be dissatisfied until the dark yesterdays of segregated schools will be transformed into bright tomorrows of quality integrated education...
>
> "There will be those moments when the buoyancy of hope will be transformed into the fatigue of despair...

"But difficult and painful as it is, we must walk on in the days ahead with an audacious faith in the future."[8]

It is that faith in the future that comes so readily when universities, whether private like ours or public like the great land-grant institutions that Lincoln first chartered, accept the challenges and the opportunities of our public missions, engaging with our communities in scholarship and education from New York to Texas, today and in the years ahead.

4

ETHICS IN THE TWENTY-FIRST CENTURY

— *Baruch A. Brody* —

Leon Jaworski Professor of Biomedical Ethics, Director of the Center
for Medical Ethics and Health Policy, Baylor College of Medicine,
Andrew Mellon Professor of Humanities, Department of Philosophy,
Rice University

My professional life has been devoted to the study, and practice, of bioethics, and this talk will focus on bioethical questions. But as my title suggests, I want to locate the discussion of bioethics within the broader context of ethics in general. There are, as far as I can see, no unique principles of bioethics; there are only bioethical applications of our general moral principles. I believe that many unacceptable bioethical views have been adopted by people who have not developed their bioethical views under the guidance of general ethical principles. For that reason, I will begin my discussion of bioethics in the twenty-first century by considering developments in ethics in general.

The above might suggest that I believe there will emerge new ethical principles in the twenty-first century to guide our bioethical thinking. That is not what I have in mind. I believe, although I cannot argue for this belief here, that ethical principles are universally true, that they hold for all people in all places at all times. In other words, I firmly oppose any form of moral relativism. But the applications of universal moral principles to ethical dilemmas may change as the circumstances to which the principles are being applied change. In this way, even a moral universalist like me can justifiably talk about a changing ethics and bioethics as we confront the evolving circumstances of the twenty-first century.

In light of these considerations, my discussion has the following structure: In the first section, I will identify three features of the twenty-first century that will challenge us to think in new ways about how our ethical principles should apply to these new circumstances. In the following sections, I will consider this question of new applications of our principles in light of each of the features I have identified as presenting us with new challenges.

Let me add one additional introductory remark. As a person of faith, I often formulate the principles and applications using theological language. I trust that this way of expressing my points will not be problematic. I do believe that the principles I will be employing can also be expressed in purely secular terms and justified by purely secular arguments, so my comments are addressed to the secular community as well. Doing so, however, loses some of the richness of expressing these principles in theological terms, and that is why I am formulating my observations using theological language.

PART I: FEATURES OF OUR NEW WORLD

The first of the features that I wish to identify is *globalization*. Globalization arises from many factors, including the following:

1. Our ability to travel long distances in comparatively short periods of time means that we encounter more of the world as we travel and that those who live in other parts of the world encounter us on a more regular basis as they travel. One simple example of the implications of global travel is the rapid spread, or concerns about possible spread, of diseases from one part of the world to another. Think of the recent scares concerning various new viruses and the resulting impact upon health care systems planning for potential catastrophic epidemics.
2. Our ability to communicate information from one part of the world to another, often by using widely available and uncontrollable means of communication, means that it is very difficult to keep information secret, and that the now publicly available information can be presented to those of us who live in other parts of the world in a very graphic and compelling manner. As one simple example of the

implications of this unfettered rapid spread of information, think of how dissidents in repressive countries are now enabled to communicate their issues and concerns to the rest of the world in ways that cannot be ignored.
3. Our ability easily to trade goods and services with other countries means that a global economic order has emerged in which our economic fates are intertwined with the fates of those who live far away from us. As I write these remarks, there is a great global concern about the sovereign debt of some countries and its implications for the economic well-being of the rest of us. This provides us with a simple example of the emergence of a truly global economic order.
4. Our scientific and technological progress is intertwined with progress in the rest of the world. Research and development have become international efforts, rather than just the efforts of a few countries. Well-trained researchers are now spread throughout the world and collaborate with their counterparts in other countries. Multinational clinical trials provide us with the simplest example of this intertwined scientific order.
5. All of these interrelated components of globalization give rise to another, perhaps deeper, feature of globalization. These other parts of the world with which the United States is increasingly interacting are shaped by cultures very different than ours, and we are challenged by issues of understanding and appropriately respecting these other cultures. Anyone who practices bioethics in a multicultural city such as Houston is well aware of the difficulties faced by providers who wish to offer culturally sensitive health care while remaining faithful to their own moral principles.

In short, God created only one world. But for most of human history, people living in one part of the world could disregard people living in other parts of the world; they were often even unaware of their existence. All this has changed, with the change occurring at a heightened pace in this century. We have to share that single world with others who are equally God's children. The first of our great challenges is how to apply our fundamental ethical principles in such a larger and more diverse world.

The second of the features that I wish to identify is the fundamental *change in the types of scientific and technological advances* that we are experiencing. Those of us who lived through much of the twentieth century are well aware of the massive scientific and technological advances of that century. But I believe that the types of changes we are now seeing are different in kind and offer the promise of even more massive developments as this century continues. Let me briefly identify these new types of changes, focusing in on the life sciences (without denying that there are other areas in which similar changes are occurring):

1. New scientific advances are increasingly growing out of a fuller understanding of our genetic composition. The fundamental knowledge made possible by the sequencing of the human genome (as well as by the comparative information provided by the sequencing of the whole genome of other animals) has laid the foundation for a new medicine based upon a scientific understanding of the genetic foundations of human traits and diseases. When this knowledge is combined with knowledge derived from large database analyses of genetic associations with diseases and treatment efficacies, we will be in a position to develop a personalized medicine, a medicine that treats your particular version of common diseases with treatments likely to be more efficacious for people with your type of genome. We are also increasingly able to identify individuals whose genetic makeup makes them more susceptible to particular diseases, so that we can identify disease early on and provide treatments that prevent or at least slow disease progression and perhaps even prevent disease onset. None of this presupposes a genetic determinism; you are obviously a product of your environment as well as your genes. What it does quite reasonably presuppose is that your genes are a major determinant of disease and cure.

2. Until now, dealing with the limitations on functioning that are the aftermath of disease has primarily been a

matter of medicines that aid functioning, rehabilitation that strengthens residual functioning, and artificial prostheses. Pressers, cardiac rehabilitation, and LVADs are examples of this approach to restoring cardiac functioning. One additional approach, developed in the last third of the twentieth century, is the transplantation of undamaged organs from donors. Regenerative medicine offers an entirely new approach to these issues. It is an attempt to use natural biological processes to restore functioning by replacing damaged tissue. If a heart attack has left you with reduced cardiac functioning because of damaged myocardium, that functioning can be restored if we can program progenitor cells to produce new cardiac tissue. This may in the end involve stem cells (adult or embryonic), but more differentiated progenitor cells might be sufficient.

3. One of the great goals of medicine is the ability to identify the onset of disease at the very earliest stage (perhaps when only a small number of cells are involved). This is not a question of disease propensity, but of actual disease onset. It is not unreasonable to suppose that very small sensors would be required to carry out such a task. Nanotechnology offers us the hope of being able to develop such sensors that could enter the body and search for these earliest diseased cells. This is, of course, not the only possibility for using nanotechnology in health care, but it is certainly one of the most exciting.

Will any of these advances actually occur? It would be foolish to be confident that they will. Think only of the example of gene transfer technology, which has yet to yield the results of genetic cures that were so confidently expected (although research still continues). But we can be confident that our century will be shaped in part by the search for these results. None of this is, of course, the reengineering of human life or the creation of posthuman persons, as some have fantasized. That would be presumptuous, at least from a theological (and perhaps even from a secular) perspective. The human features being exploited and mechanisms being proposed are ones imposed by God as part of the natural order. But it certainly is based upon an investigation into God's order at a far more fundamental level, something that has seemed objectionable to some. I have not, however, been able to understand what these objections really are.

The third of the features that I wish to identify is *the recognition of human limitations and of inevitable finitude*. Religious people have always understood that infinitude is a feature only of God. Everything else is finite, and this finitude imposes limitations. I believe that the twenty-first century is going to be the century in which these messages are brought home to us, and that this is going to impact profoundly our thinking. Let us consider just three examples:

1. One of the most important drivers of this recognition will be the emergence of demands from rapidly developing countries (e.g., India and China) with large populations. As the incomes of these populations grow, they become competitors for so many of the resources whose abundant use is central to our own prosperity. We already see this in a simple way in the rising prices of various commodities. But there are other more complex and perhaps more important examples. Consider the question of personnel engaged in scientific research. Everyone involved in that enterprise knows how dependent many laboratories are upon foreign graduate students and post-docs, and how many of the best of them stay in the United States to continue their research. But as their home countries increase their scientific and educational funding and infrastructure, fewer trainees will feel the need to come and, among those who come, many more will return home. Notice that we are not considering here limitations in total numbers, but rather an increasing sense of limitation in countries that have felt less limited in the past, as some of those resources and personnel go elsewhere. No doubt, more commodities can be discovered and more researchers can be trained, but there are limitations to these possibilities. Even if this is seen as a legitimate balancing of the availability of such commodities and human resources among different countries, it will still challenge us to develop new approaches to

meaning as we come to recognize that we cannot count on what we have had in the past.

2. There are other examples in which a sense of absolute finitude will increasingly develop. There are cases where we will increasingly face total limitations. Perhaps the most pressing examples relate to fundamental commodities such as clean air and clean water. Those who have emphasized sustainable development have seen these issues emerging for some time, but all of us will see them to a greater degree as the twenty-first century progresses. I want to make it clear that this point does not depend upon adopting a particular view about controversial questions such as the global warming debate. The problem I am raising goes beyond any specific example.

3. Then there is the question of limitations on healthy and satisfactory longevity. The twentieth century was marked by a tremendous expansion in life expectancy throughout the world (with the greatest growth being in countries where life expectancy was quite low). Moreover, developments in medicine have led to more people living those extra years in better health and increased functioning, even though this is balanced by the increased number of people living their last years in states of physical disability and/or dementia. But how far can this extension continue? No one knows the answer to that question, and no one also knows what will be the impact of any slowdown on our psyche. There is a larger issue here; the need to find meaningfulness in those extra years. All of us who are getting closer to the age of retirement yearn for that increased freedom, but many of us wonder what can give those years full meaning. There is a famous philosophical essay called "The Tedium of Immortality." For many, the fear is the tedium of those last twenty years of life. Can we offer a more expansive understanding of meaningful and fulfilling life to all those who will have more healthy years to live, or is the human capacity for meaning limited in that way?

Malthus was wrong in his prophecies of doom. Technological advances will certainly alleviate some of these limitations. But it is an act of theological hubris to suppose that these issues of finitude and limitations can be solved by technological fixes. In the end, only God is infinite. Moreover, the larger issues will be those of the human spirit as we confront the questions of meaning that cannot be solved technologically.

PART II: The Ethical and Beoethical Impacts of Globalization

I turn now to examples of how globalization impacts upon our thinking about ethical issues, even if the principles we employ remain the same. The examples I will use in this part refer to structural issues surrounding the provision of health care. They are not necessarily examples that immediately come to mind when thinking about ethical issues, but they are to my mind crucial where globalization calls for new perspectives.

My first example has to do with pharmaceuticals. One of the crucial features of medicine as it developed in the second half of the twentieth century was its increasingly heavy reliance on medications whose safety and efficacy have been established in scientific research. We take for granted that there will be medicines for treating conditions such as infections, heart failure, diabetes, and cancer. We anticipate that there will in the future be medicines for currently untreatable diseases such as dementia. Few of us can remember the time before World War II when efficacious and safe medications were scarce, but most of us can remember the excitement when new classes of drugs to treat new conditions were developed and approved.

None of this happens effortlessly. New drugs that might work must first be identified (often only after extensive basic scientific research suggests possibilities for these new drugs), rigorously tested in animals and then in humans, and approved after a lengthy review process. This course of research and development is a very expensive one. It has been estimated that it costs on average $800 million to bring a new drug to market. Whether or not this figure is correct or an overestimate, no one can doubt that the costs are extensive. The scientists who do the research may be rewarded for their efforts by professional recognition and promotion to better positions, as well as by a sense of real achievement. But those who invest in the process of research and development expect, and seem entitled to, a financial reward. That reward is granted by patents, which give an exclusive right to produce and sell the newly approved drug for a limited period of time. The thought is that companies will price the drug for that period of time in a way that offers adequate rewards for their past investments and adequate incentives for future investments. Acceptance of this system is based upon a capitalistic ethic that supports incentives to invest and rewards for successful investment. Some see this as just an economic reality. I see it as an expression of a social philosophy and a social ethics that is foundational to societies based upon market economies—a social philosophy and ethics that I support.

There is, of course, another side to this story. The whole point of developing these new pharmaceuticals is to make better treatments available to those in need of them—*all* of those in need of them. Some justify this claim by reference to a right to health care. I have no objection to that, but I think that it is ethically superior to make drugs available to those in need of them as a compassionate response by society based upon recognizing that all of us are equally created in God's image and all of us are equally his children. So this other side of the story is also rooted in a fundamental moral philosophy and social ethics. To accommodate both of these points, we have developed a variety of mechanisms, including limiting the time of the patent and insurance mechanisms to pay the cost of the pharmaceuticals in early years. Globalization transforms this discussion in two major ways:

- Our global system of communicating information, one of the aspects of globalization noted above, has made us very aware of how many people are in need of these pharmaceuticals in other parts of the world. This message has been made clear through the crisis of how to make antiretrovirals available to those suffering in very poor countries, but it is not unique to that problem (think of TB, malaria, childhood diarrhea, and others). The call of compassion has been met in a number of ways. The Global Fund, as an international response, and PEPFAR, as a U.S. response, have made a great deal of money available for purchasing and supplying these drugs, and negotiations between NGOs and the pharmaceutical industry and modifications of TRIPS patent protection have lessened the costs of these drugs in poor countries while preserving corporate profits and incentives. All of this is an attempt to accommodate both of our moral commitments. But the majority of those in need of such drugs throughout the world are still not receiving them. Some would say this means we just have to spend more money. But this neglects the importance of a sense of finitude and limitations. There are many needs, and we must ask how this should be prioritized. How to apply our commitments to capitalistic incentives and to compassionate care of those in need, in the context of a global community well aware of the limitations on its capacities, is my first example of how globalization is calling us in the twenty-first century to develop a more nuanced understanding of our ethical principles as they apply to pharmaceuticals.

- While this issue has been widely discussed, there is another issue related to globalization and pharmaceuticals that deserves more attention. Another aspect of globalization is the emergence of a truly global economic order. Pharmaceutical manufacturers are international enterprises selling their products throughout the world. It is easy to adopt the stance that they should sell their pharmaceuticals at very low prices (perhaps not more than the cost of production) in very poor countries; they have nothing to lose because they couldn't sell them in those countries at higher prices. It is also easy to adopt the stance that their return on investments must come primarily from sales in affluent countries that can use insurance schemes to cover the costs to patients in need. But how should those pharmaceuticals be priced in rapidly developing countries? Some might argue that such countries still need the same low prices so that they can use their funds to promote development. Others might argue that it is time for them to pay a fair share to cover the full costs of research and development, keeping in mind that a fair share might still be considerably less than the share paid by affluent countries. A new ethical question emerges here. One of our other moral principles is a commitment to everyone doing their fair share. How do we understand fair share in this complex area?

To summarize, we have long-standing ethical commitments to capitalistic incentives, to compassion in ensuring access, and to fairness. Globalization offers us new challenges to applying these principles in a global economic order well aware of its limitations and finitude.

My second example of the impact of globalization has to do with conducting research, and using its results, in morally controversial areas when the controversy is perceived very differently in different parts of the global scientific order. I will use as my example stem cell research and the development of regenerative medicine.

There are certain points that are uncontroversial: (1) regenerative medicine offers the hope for cures, or at least ameliorations, of many diseases that currently cannot be properly treated; (2) research on basic issues is needed immediately, and then there will be a need for an extensive process of development of treatments; (3) all of this research, and the eventual treatments, require the use of progenitor cells; (4) it is not yet known whether differentiated progenitor cells will be sufficient, whether adult stem cells will be required, or whether embryonic stem cells would be required; (5) from a scientific perspective, the obvious strategy would be to permit and fund research using all of these progenitor cells, but there are moral issues that need to be considered; (6) as things stand, research using embryonic stem cells requires the destruction of living early embryos existing ex utero; (7) moral attitudes within the United States range from those who see such acts of destruction as the murder of living human beings to those who see the process as morally unproblematic and even mandatory in our search for the cure of diseases; (8) the same debate is occurring throughout the world, but there are many countries that see no real problems with such research, and among those countries are emerging scientific powers, some of whom are also economic rivals of the United States; this is part of what globalization and its resulting cultural variances mean; (9) the results of whatever research and development are done using embryonic stem cells will be known throughout the world, and if that approach turns out to be particularly available, Americans will certainly want the resulting treatments; all of this is part of globalization in the communication of information; (10) medical tourism is already an established fact, and if effective treatments are available outside the United States but not in the United States, Americans will travel to get them; this is what globalization in travel means.

As the potential for regenerative medicine using embryonic stem cells and other progenitor cells emerged at the end of the twentieth century, two debates broke out in the United States. The first debate centered on the morality of this research. Was it inherently evil? Did it make a difference whether the research was conducted on spare embryos from reproductive medicine clinics that would otherwise be destroyed? And so forth? The second debate centered on issues of moral pluralism. How should a social policy be structured for a society in which people disagreed at such a fundamental level about the morality of this research? Should the research be supported only by private funds, without the use of any public funds? Should the research be allowed at all? Should these questions be answered differently in different states, given the variability in cultural differences among states and given the American commitment to federalism? We are all familiar with how this second type of debate played out in the political arena, with Presidents Bush and Obama taking very different positions. I will not say anything more about those debates here. Instead, I want to raise a series of ethical questions about regenerative medicine growing out of points 8–10, the points about globalization of research, of knowledge, and of travel.

One of the questions I want to raise concerns the implications of the fact that the research will be done anyway. Given that fact, many have argued that it is wrong to put the United States behind other countries both scientifically and economically. If, of course, other progenitor cells turn out to be as good as embryonic stem cells, the loss to the United States scientific community and economy from not engaging in embryonic stem cell research will not be that great. But if embryonic stem cells turn out to be superior, then the loss to the United States will be much greater. In short, these people argue, a restrictive United States policy accomplishes nothing except disadvantaging the country from both a scientific and an ethical perspective. So even those who have moral objections to destructive stem cell research should allow for a social policy of funding such research. Others don't see it that way. They believe that destructive embryonic stem cell research is inherently immoral, and ask why the United States should fund or even allow such immoral research just because others are doing it. They also argue that if we lose some benefits by adhering to our moral principles, we also gain by adhering to our moral principles.

The globalization of this policy issue has brought even greater complexity to the question of moral pluralism. We all support the principle that people should not violate the dictates of their conscience. We all support the principle that we must accept and respect the reality of moral pluralism in developing social policy. That is why there is a certain attraction to the view that we should allow, but not publicly fund, embryonic stem cell research. (I do not claim that this is the correct position—I am only claiming that it is an attractive position.) But the question of national scientific and economic competitiveness complicates things when the world contains countries that have no reason to limit public support because there is no significant public opposition to the research.

The other question I want to raise concerns the provision of regenerative medical services as part of public insurance plans. We have had a long-standing debate in the United States about the public funding of abortions. But it is important to keep in mind that abortions, however important they are for those who believe in them, are not the treatment of an illness (except, perhaps, when the continued pregnancy threatens the life or health of the mother). Regenerative treatments, even if they involve destroying early embryos ex utero, are treatments of illnesses. This raises the question of whether it is just to deny those who are on public insurance the benefits of those treatments if they involve destroying embryos, while the more affluent can receive them (by paying for them or by having them covered by private insurance plans). This question would, of course, be present without any issues of globalization. But imagine the heightened sense of injustice felt by those not receiving these treatments in the United States while citizens of other countries have equal access. On the other hand, opponents of such treatments would argue that public funding would mean that their moral integrity would be violated because they would be required to support indirectly that which they think is inherently immoral.

The question of developing social policies for pluralistic societies is a notoriously complex issue that predates any issues of globalization. What I have suggested is that globalization complicates things further because it raises issues of global competitiveness and of global injustices. The twenty-first century will have to deal with these additional complexities. Remember, however, that this does not mean that we need new moral principles. What it does mean is that the application of our principles is going to be more complex as a result of globalization.

PART III: The Ethical and Bioethical Implications of Radically New Types of Sciences

There are many examples of new bioethical issues raised by these recent scientific developments. I want to focus on one set of issues—those related to more accurate predictive knowledge about our health-related futures. This knowledge will raise new ethical dilemmas for individuals, health care providers, and society as a whole.

Human beings are mortal creatures; all of us will die. But for most of human history, we have had very crude ways of predicting our medical future. Some diseases ran in certain families, so members of those families knew that they were more likely to develop that disease. Women with a strong family history of breast cancer and anyone with a strong family history of colon cancer knew that they were at a higher risk of developing those diseases. These predictive tools were what made family history such a crucial component of the medical history taken by physicians and also the underwriting activities of life insurance companies. But what made all of this so crude was the fact that only some family members developed the relevant diseases; others did not, and people really had no way of knowing which outcome they would have. Moreover, many people developed these diseases without any family history. Also, some diseases were more prevalent in certain environments, so people living in one of those environments knew that they were at greater risk of developing those diseases. But this was also a crude predictive device, because many people living in the same environment did not develop the disease, and again one had no way of knowing which outcome they would have. And of course many people developed the disease while not living in such environments. The same holds true for predicting disease (e.g., lung cancer) on the basis of behavioral risks (e.g., smoking).

Things began to change at the end of the twentieth century as our knowledge of the genetic component of diseases increased exponentially. We will use as our example the genetics of breast cancer. All women are at risk for breast cancer (12% will develop it during their lifetime). But only 2% of women have a serious family history of breast cancer (a sufficient number of close enough family members), so most breast cancers develop in women without a serious family history. Moreover, according to a 2008 study, while a serious family history means a four-fold increase in breast cancer risk, the majority of women with such a family history do not develop breast cancer. But with the discovery of two genetic mutations (BRCA1 and BRCA2), the whole nature of prediction began to change. Most (60%–80%) of women with one of those mutations develop breast cancer during their lifetimes. As a result, women in high-risk populations (and even some who are not in such populations) are being tested and many of those who test positively for the mutations have begun taking medicines prophylactically. Some have even undergone mastectomies and oophrectomies to lessen their risk.

This general pattern is likely to be repeated regularly in the twenty-first century: Susceptibility for many diseases is clearly related to family history. But the majority of people with the positive family history do not develop the disease, and most people who develop the disease do not have the positive family history. Then a genetic mutation is discovered that correlates with the disease. A negative test for the mutation is still of no significance; a person still has a good chance of developing the disease because most people who have the disease do not have the mutation. But a positive test for the mutation is of great significance, for those who test positively are highly likely to develop the disease. Preventive treatments will emerge for these people, but they will often involve medications with serious side effects or major surgeries. Facing this pattern of events, patients, health care providers, and society will confront new ethical challenges:

Issues for the patient. As long as there are no effective ways of slowing the onset of the disease and/or treating it when it develops, the question of being tested to determine whether one is at risk or even certain to develop the disease is really a matter of personal feelings. Consider the case of Huntington's chorea. If a person has the wrong genes, he or she will develop this disease, and there is nothing that can be done. Because the disease manifests itself in middle age, unless one is tested genetically one will not know whether the disease will develop until it emerges. Some people at risk prefer not to know, concerned that the knowledge will emotionally cloud their lives in early, healthy years. Others prefer to know, thinking that the knowledge can help them plan how to use the good time that they have. Perhaps the only real ethical issue is about whether to choose to reproduce, knowing the risks to future children. Contrast this with the genetics of breast cancer and the many other examples coming down the road. Moreover, suppose one believes that people have a moral responsibility to care for their bodies and their health. Religious people express this theme as the idea that we are God's steward over our bodies. Secularly, we can treat this as an obligation we have to ourselves as part of our duty to respect human dignity. What are our moral obligations to test ourselves for disease susceptibility? How far are we obliged to adopt measures to prevent or delay the onset of disease or to screen so as to allow for early treatment? Or is this at the end just a matter of personal choice because we have no such obligations? These issues will become ever more pressing in the twenty-first century, as they probe the meaning of the obligation to care for one's health.

Issues for health care providers. Providers should not, and usually cannot, force their patients to make particular health care decisions, but they certainly are entitled (perhaps even required) to encourage their patients to make those decisions that are good for their health. This is a fundamental part of the physician's obligation of fidelity to the interests of the patient. Recent research has identified the extensive ways in which more than encouragement takes place. The way physicians structure the choice decision, the way they present information, and the system of defaults they adopt nudge patients in one direction or another. This realization has led to a series of fascinating new moral questions. How much should physicians limit or exploit this phenomenon when dealing with these decisions? Consider the physician who is discussing genetic screening for breast cancer susceptibility with patients who have serious family histories. Should the physician treat such screening as what is done unless the patient objects? Should the physician treat such screening as something that is done only if the patient requests it? Is there a third, more neutral way? These questions have been endemic to the patient-physician relation ever since crude paternalism was rejected in the second half of the twentieth century. But they are even more pressing in our century when the issue is genetic testing (with its implications for more than the patient) and when the techniques of nudging are better understood. What does the obligation of fidelity to the interests of the patient mean in our century?

Issues for society. There are many social issues, but I want to focus on one. We have as a society traditionally not allowed patient access to any diagnostic or therapeutic intervention that someone is willing to supply. New drugs and devices (including diagnostic devices) must be approved by a regulatory agency before they can be offered for use. So there is a certain acceptance of social paternalism built into our system. For a variety of technical reasons, much of the new genetic testing is available without any regulatory approval; I anticipate that this will change over time, as new types of concerns about efficacy and safety emerge. But these new concerns about safety and efficacy are going to be of a very different nature. They are going to relate, for example, to safety issues caused by reliance upon genetic information whose predictive value is yet unclear. Imagine someone undergoing a preventive mastectomy on the basis of a genetic predictor of breast disease that is much less validated than BRCA1 or BRCA2. To use the validation of the predictive value of a genetic test as a criterion for its social approval is to have society making judgments about the reliability of information, and that goes against our fundamental commitment to freedom in the flow of information. The conflict between freedom in the flow of information and social paternalism will be heightened as new genetic information becomes available.

To summarize, the proliferation in the twenty-first century of genetic information related to disease susceptibility is going to lead to a rethinking of such traditional moral beliefs as stewardship over one's body, fidelity to the interests of patients, freedom in the flow of information, and legitimate social paternalism. These moral principles will not lose their validity, but our understanding of them will be more nuanced as we apply them to the complexities of genetic information available in this century.

PART IV: THE ETHICAL AND BIOETHICAL IMPLICATIONS OF THE INCREASING RECOGNITION OF HUMAN LIMITATIONS AND OF INEVITABLE FINITUDE

The twentieth century was a century in which everything seemed possible, even though it was at the same time a century of terrible horrors. Science and technology were advancing on so many fronts, and it seemed possible to envisage a far better (although hardly perfect) world in which so much human misery would be overcome by the application of scientifically driven technologies. Much of this has in fact occurred. To give just one example, think of the tremendous increase in life expectancy throughout the world. But what I will now suggest is that our sense of optimism must in this century be tempered by a recognition of our limitations and finitude; the resulting nuanced view of the future will give rise to new questions of priorities and of meaning.

I will begin my discussion by reflecting on the delivery of health care in the United States. The United States has been the leader in scientific research and its applications to medical practice and new technology, although that position is now being challenged due to the impact of globalization, as discussed above. But the use of these new medical discoveries is one of the major drivers of increased health care expenditures. I always like to think of this issue in terms of the percentage of gross domestic product devoted to health care. It was not too long ago that 10% was the relevant figure, but we are now much closer to 18%, and 20% seems likely within the not-too-distant future; a good deal of this increase is due to the adoption of expensive new technologies.

I do not intend here to focus on the features of our health care system that might be modified to lessen such growth in expenditures. Instead, I want to focus on ethical issues confronting us even if we were to modify those features. However modified, there will always remain the drive to add new life-enhancing and life-expanding treatments that add costs to the system. Some root this drive in the sanctity of human life. I prefer not to do so, because I have theological doubts about the use of the language of sanctity as applied to human life. It is sufficient, I think, to root such access to treatment in a commitment to the preciousness of human life (grounded, from a theological perspective, in a belief that all humans are created in the image of God). So when new and very expensive treatments come along that can extend human life for a few months or even just improve its quality for a few months, we think it worthwhile to spend that money.

Allow me to digress for a moment to pay tribute to Cardinal Bernadine, whose concept of a consistent ethics of life has greatly influenced my thinking and deserves more attention than it has received. Addressing himself to a pro-life community, he called upon them to be consistent in their commitment to the preciousness of human life. That means not only protecting the life of those unborn, but also protecting the lives of those already born who are threatened by disease but lack access to the medical care they need. It is this seamless value that has driven our commitment to the expansion of treatments we provide, or at least should provide, to all in need of them.

It is this fundamental value that needs to be nuanced by our recognition of human limitations and finitude. That recognition grows out of our reflections on the percentage of GDP devoted to health care. It is not a question of economics but rather a question of the balancing of values when we think about the resources available to us. Economists have introduced the important concept of opportunity costs. Money that is spent on one good thing is not available to spend on other good things; you lose some opportunities when you spend money on other opportunities. Health care is, of course, not the only thing of value, even if we think of extending human life. Eliminating environmental threats to health, greater safety in the workplace and in our infrastructure, and general education and especially education about how to be healthy are all effective ways of extending human lives, but they also cost money. And once we add the value of enhancing human life, still more good opportunities on which to spend our money emerge.

This is, of course, not a problem that we face uniquely in the United States. All countries face it to a greater or lesser degree. Some have confronted it more directly than we have. But I am not necessarily satisfied with how they have dealt with this issue. There was a time when the United Kingdom denied dialysis to those over 55, and it has in place today mechanisms to limit the use of expensive treatments that provide only modest extensions of life. These are the sorts of examples that raised concerns (even if, as I believe, they were misguided) about "death panels" in recent U.S. debate. My concern is not with the outcomes of the U.K. process, but with its nature. What we need is not a process that focuses solely on how best to spend our health care dollars. What we need instead is a far broader process based on a democratic dialogue about our values and how we prioritize them.

Am I saying that the growing recognition and acceptance of the finitude and limitations of human capacities require health care rationing? No! What I am saying is that such recognition and acceptance call for a far-reaching dialogue about the prioritization of values. Keep in mind that such a process might prioritize health care so much that we decide to limit expenditures in other areas. After all, one of the values at the top of the list will certainly be the preciousness of human life. The dialogue for which I am calling may conclude that this value has such a priority that we cannot in any way ration health care or other measures that extend life; any rationing due to our finitude would have to take place in other areas. Or it may conclude that the preciousness of human life has considerable priority but not absolute priority; some forms of health care might have to be rationed in order to make possible the promotion of other values. The ethical task of our century is to conduct a dialogue about the priority of our values, a dialogue based upon our acceptance of limitations and finitude. It would be presumptuous of myself or anyone else to claim to know what the result of that dialogue would, or should, be.

That, of course, leads us to a very different and difficult ethical challenge, the question of how to design such a dialogue and implement its results. As we reflect on that question, there is one crucial threshold point that must be kept in mind. Much of the prioritizing depends on how individuals order their own values as they decide how to spend their limited, finite resources. These may just be private choices, at least as long as the choices do not harm other individuals. But even here there is much that needs to be said from an ethical perspective. Although individuals are entitled to spend their resources as they see fit, this does not mean that their decisions are just a matter of choice and that ethics has nothing to say about the respective merits of those private choices. There has been much confusion between saying that such issues are personal choices and saying that any choice a person makes is equally good from an ethical perspective. Classical virtue theory understood that some of those personal choices reflected, and reinforced, the virtuous life. We need to recover that sense of virtuous choice and apply it to thinking about how we choose among the limited options available to us when we make private choices. This is central to living a meaningful life.

Having said that, we must also remember that there still is a need to address the mechanisms for determining priorities in the expenditure of social resources. There are, of course, two questions here: (1) How much of what we produce should be treated as social resources? This is, of course, the fundamental question of tax theory. Even before a society decides who should be taxed—and how much in order to reach a certain targeted goal of tax revenue—it must decide what that amount should be. (2) How should the tax revenues be spent? What values should receive priority—and how much priority—when we are confronting the question of limited resources?

I hope no one expects that I will now announce the answer to those questions. When I was younger, I actually envisaged developing a theory of just taxation that simultaneously resolved both of these questions. Young people are entitled to grandiose goals, but that approach becomes presumptuous and even foolish in more mature people. I think we need to give up the hope that we can develop a universally valid answer to those two questions. At most, we can hope to develop a reasonable and ethically acceptable process for answering them at any given time.

Let me be clear about what I have been claiming. The preciousness of human life remains as valid a value as it always has been. There are, of course, other legitimate important values. In the latter part of the twentieth century, many affluent countries (especially the United

States) operated under the seductive assumption that we could have it all, disregarding the finitude of the human condition. This was an act of hubris. The growing percentage of the GDP devoted to health care, due in a significant degree to the desire to extend that precious human life, should now remind us of our limitations and finitude. This is not a call to changing our values. It is a call to adopt a more nuanced understanding of our values in a world in which prioritization should be seen as a necessary consequence of human finitude.

PART V: CONCLUSION

There are many fundamental values and moral principles involved in the ethical and bioethical issues I have discussed. Some of these include the following:

- Compassion in meeting the needs of others
- Respect for the preciousness of human life
- Recognition of the inherent finitude of human beings
- Respect for the need to accommodate moral pluralism
- Fairness in the distribution of joint burdens
- Belief in the legitimate rewards of capitalistic investment
- Obligations of stewardship over our body
- Fidelity to the interests of those with whom we stand in special relations.

None of these are new values; I believe they are universally valid principles and values that have long been recognized by people sensitive to the truths of morality.

I have not claimed that globalization, new types of scientific and technological advances, and the increased recognition of human finitude will challenge the legitimacy of these values. What I have claimed is that we will need to develop a more nuanced understanding of these values, and how they interact with each other in changed circumstances, if we are to meet the ethical challenges of the twenty-first century.

5

THE CHALLENGES AND OPPORTUNITIES FOR LIBERAL EDUCATION IN A FAITH-BASED UNIVERSITY

— *Lee S. Shulman* —

Charles E. Ducommun Professor of Education Emeritus and Professor of Psychology Emeritus, Stanford University, President Emeritus, Carnegie Foundation for the Advancement of Teaching

In what manner can a faculty and student body pursue liberal education in a faith-based university? To many who think about such matters, the juxtaposition of "liberal" education and a "faith-based" or "Christian" university appears to be a contradiction in terms. Liberal education rests on a commitment to doubt, skepticism, openness to a broad spectrum of views without prejudgment, a rejection of dogma and an insistence on evidence and continuous inquiry. In contrast, a life "based on faith" is built upon a commitment to eternal, divinely inspired and revealed truth that takes precedence over doubt and skepticism, setting limits to inquiry and boundaries around investigation.

My argument in this essay is that no contradiction need exist between these two commitments. This is not to say that the intersection of faith and liberal learning lacks contentiousness. On the contrary, it can be a dauntingly difficult marriage, but out of the challenge may develop a deeper and more profoundly liberally educated citizen in a democracy than may emerge from institutions that lack this testing ground, that are not home to that educational crucible where both the liberal and the faithful intersect, collide, and, under the best conditions, become mutually enriching.

Thus my attitude toward the confluence of liberal education and faith-based education is akin to the philosophy articulated by my predecessor as Carnegie Foundation president, the late John Gardner, when he first addressed his staff on becoming Secretary of Health, Education, and Welfare in 1964: "We are confronted with a set of unlimited opportunities masquerading as insoluble problems." I believe that in a context like Baylor, where liberalizing faith-based education and sanctifying liberal education define the essence of its pedagogical mission, this confluence of challenge and opportunity is striking.

I too come from a background in which the intersection of religious and secular studies was a feature of everyday life. In my middle school and high school years growing up in Chicago, I was educated at an Orthodox Jewish day school and yeshiva where I was immersed for nearly four hours every day in the study of sacred texts, primarily Talmud and Bible in their original Hebrew and Aramaic. The prime morning hours were devoted to those studies, and the afternoons, when we students might have been a tad less alert, were dedicated to English, math, history, the sciences, and foreign languages. At the age of sixteen I was admitted to the college of the University of Chicago and at that point I became a yeshiva dropout. Somewhat ironically, in beginning my undergraduate studies at Chicago where the Great Books curriculum replaced the Torah and the Talmud as sacred texts, many of the habits of mind and strategies of textual interpretation transferred over with remarkable ease. This experience of moving between the university and yeshiva worlds and the modes of thought and commitment that characterize each of those cultures has been a significant influence on the thinking that animates the present essay. And while the professional focus of my life has since been that of secular academia, I continue to study the Jewish sources regularly and find in them a source of inspiration and enlightenment.

Three Stories

There is a sound homiletic axiom that stories are the best pathway to understanding. In that spirit, I shall offer you three accounts that will serve to introduce the central arguments I shall make in this essay.

The Trip to Messiah

Nearly fifteen years ago I was returning from one of my frequent visits to Jerusalem and flying to Philadelphia in order to give a talk at a superb undergraduate Christian institution, Messiah College. Messiah had been the alma mater of my predecessor as president of the Carnegie Foundation, the late Ernest Boyer, and I was scheduled to give a lecture in his memory. My plane was late, a connection was missed, and I didn't land in Philadelphia until 3 a.m. Waiting for me was a young man who introduced himself as a Messiah graduate, now working in the admissions office while waiting for his future wife to finish her degree. As we made the early morning drive across Pennsylvania, I asked about his plans. He had been a religion major, and I suppose I was expecting him to describe his intention to attend a seminary where he might be ordained as a minister.

He explained that he had been admitted to Yale Divinity School, where he would begin his graduate program the following fall. My silence must have been audible. "You seem surprised by my plans," he said softly. I mumbled something about whether he was anxious about the likelihood that the students and faculty members at Yale would approach the reading of sacred texts rather differently than he might be accustomed to. He chuckled and replied that I clearly did not understand how students at Messiah College were taught to read Scripture. He explained that he, like most entering students at Messiah College, had come from a home in which they had practiced only one way of reading the Bible, and that was to read it in a "devotional" manner. As a Messiah graduate he had learned a most important lesson. He had learned at Messiah to read Scripture "both devotionally and critically without losing the capacity for either." I have never forgotten that exchange or his succinct and powerful way of articulating the transformative impact of his education. To read and think both devotionally and critically without losing the capacity to do either serves as a statement of the argument of this chapter and the goals of liberal education in a faith-based university. In a homiletic sense, his words could serve as my text. "I learned I could read both devotionally and critically without losing my capacity for either."

The Power of Argument: machloket

When in 2004 we inaugurated the new building for the Carnegie Foundation, a beautiful structure perched high on a hill overlooking Stanford University and San Francisco Bay, I invited two good friends—a minister and a rabbi—to participate in the dedication ceremony. When we met together, they asked if I had a favorite scriptural passage that I would like them to use in their joint ceremony. Instead, I suggested my favorite rabbinical aphorism: *"Talmidei chachamim marbim shalom ba'olam,"* which translates as "Sages increase peace in the world." I found it particularly appropriate at the dedication of a center for educational scholarship, policy, and action that I had dubbed a "habitat for thought" during the long period of planning and design that preceded construction of the building.

Rabbi Abraham Isaac Kook, in his commentary on the Hebrew liturgy, made the wry observation that this verse served as proof that the rabbis of the Talmud had a sense of humor. For what could be funnier than the claim that scholars promote peace in the world? Do not scholars constantly engage in arguments with one another about nearly everything? They argue about the proper interpretation of a sacred text, about the correct sequence of actions in the liturgy of a holy day, or about the right way to observe particular items of Jewish religious law ("*halacha*"). Scholars don't create *shalom*, peace; they foster *machloket*, disagreement or argument. They divide members of a community into warring parties rather than unifying the community in the interests of peace. Scholars foment disagreement and dissension.

Not so, argued the eminent rabbinical scholar. Properly to understand the verse requires that we grasp the etymological sources of the two key words, *shalom* and *machloket*, peace and argument. The term *machloket* is generally defined as "argument" but literally derives from the Hebrew "*chelek*," which means a piece, a "part of a whole." A *machloket* is a disagreement in which each advocate has taken a piece of the complex totality of an issue and has rested his argument on the validity of that piece. All those whose views are divided in argument are thought to play necessary roles in the pursuit of truth because each opposing view holds a portion of the whole.

Similarly, there are several senses of *shalom*—not only peace, but more literally fullness, completion, integrity. Peace occurs when all the pieces fall into place, when the parts are brought together in harmony. All the parts of a disagreement are necessary in a *machloket*, because no single interpretation or opinion, however large, prestigious, or central, is sufficient. An important analogy is that resolving an argument is like putting together one of those old large jigsaw puzzles for which, even as you begin, you suspect that you may not have all the pieces. Nevertheless, you keep working on it, hoping that by some miracle or good fortune, the pieces will somehow all fit together.

In that important sense, argument and disagreement are the necessary prerequisites to the accomplishment of *shalom*, of a full, ever more complete, rich and comprehensive grasp of truth. Without *machloket* we can achieve only an illusion of truth, a fantasy of *shalom*. Only through *machloket* can "*shalom*" emerge.

In the spirit of Rabbi Kook, I define a liberally educated person as someone capable of treating texts and their ideas so seriously that they are taken as sacred. And a text that is viewed as sacred is approached with the kind of reverence and attention that obligates the reader, he or she who encounters the text, to approach that text with such deep devotion that the text can be heard crying out for interpretation, commentary, richly alternative understandings, and, yes, celebrations of its unavoidable ambiguities. Indeed, in all fields, the more central and essential an idea becomes for its domain—whether theology, biology, or politics—the more uncertain and ambiguous is its interpretation. The more an idea needs to bear the burden of essentiality, the more it demands from those who revere and study it a discipline of concentration, perseverance, and patient study, along with a tolerance for ambiguity and an openness to alternative interpretations. We do not have a right to claim understanding of a sacred text until we have sought alternative interpretations that may throw our own favorite into doubt. We do not treat these other views as alien; we search for them as precious aids to understanding. This is a preference, to presage some ideas we will encounter shortly, for "a hermeneutic of reserved judgment" rather than "a hermeneutic of suspicion."

Referring to the Hebrew Bible, the rabbis assert, "turn it and turn it yet again for everything can be found in it." To call something ambiguous is not to claim that it is trivial or vacuous. On the contrary, it carries multiple meanings because so few words and sentences will be called upon to resonate with so many life experiences and to serve as vessels of meaning under circumstances that range far beyond those found in the plain meaning of the text.[1]

Robert Putnam's American Grace

My third encounter was with a fine new book, *American Grace*,[2] a study of religion in America, by the eminent political scientist Robert Putnam. In an interview Putnam gave at Stanford during the year the book was published, Putnam reported the volume's main ideas:

> America is a very religious country. The statistics in the book show the average American is more religious than the average Iranian. That has powerful effects on our civic life, both dividing us and uniting us. America is very unusual in the sense that we're religiously devout, religiously diverse and actually quite religiously tolerant. Very few places in the world are all three of those.

I found the coexistence of these three attributes quite stunning. Indeed, one could offer the argument that the impact of a faith-based university with a strong commitment to liberal education would be a population of religiously devout members of their faith community who were simultaneously actively tolerant and accepting of people and ideas emanating from other faiths. To the extent that our educational mission is to prepare civically engaged and responsible leaders who can be seriously committed to their own religious beliefs and also participate fully in the discourse and debates of a democratic society, Putnam's three findings are not simply interesting; they are the ingredients needed for the functioning of the kind of democratic society we have in the United States whose survival and flourishing are central goals of higher education.

THE ATTRIBUTES OF A LIBERALLY EDUCATED PERSON (LEP)

My colleagues at the Carnegie Foundation, Anne Colby, Thomas Ehrlich, William Sullivan, and Jon Dolle, have coauthored a book on the role of liberal learning in the preparation of business leaders,

Rethinking Undergraduate Business Education: Liberal Learning for the Profession.[3] As I prepared to write the foreword to that book, a role I played for each of the two dozen volumes of research and policy analysis that we completed at the Carnegie Foundation during my presidency, it became clear that this was a book not only about preparation for business (even though the business major is the most popular undergraduate concentration in America). It is a treatment of the role of liberal learning in preparing any undergraduate student for civic engagement, practicing membership in a learned profession, the life of a scholar and teacher in the academic worlds of elementary, secondary, or higher education.

The authors present the thesis that liberal education equips the future citizen with three kinds of capacity. The first is a capacity for analytic and critical thinking, reading, and reasoning. The second is a capacity for seeking and developing multiple perspectives on important questions. The third is a disposition and capacity to use those deep understandings enriched by a sense of multiplicity of dimension and perspective, to achieve personal meaning, to form a significant sense of self or identity, and to develop abiding commitments and a sense of devotion in one's own life.

I thus see a liberally educated person as someone who can engage complex texts deeply and interpretively, and be capable of engaging hermeneutically with demanding texts, ideas, and artifacts. This is terribly important in a faith-based setting because the big ideas of theology, social science, and natural science are inherently complex, ambiguous, and typically incomplete and incomprehensible without interpretation. For all practical purposes, "plain meaning" is illusory when dealing with the truly central writings and ideas. Each individual should become personally equipped to read and interpret these texts.

The second attribute of the liberally educated person is the capacity to address complex problems from multiple perspectives. This does not mean that the learner is ultimately always a relativist, always saying "on the one hand" and "on the other hand." The liberally educated person is capable of understanding positions that are not her own, is disposed to consider them carefully and sympathetically, and is respectful of those who hold those positions, looking carefully to understand their arguments, their evidence, and the consequences of their conclusions. Moreover, the liberally educated person recognizes that opposing ideas are likely to enrich one's understanding even as they vex it, and therefore seeks out and relishes those enrichments rather than avoiding or censoring them. The liberally educated person values *machloket*.

The third attribute of the liberally educated person is that he or she is someone whose interpretations, perspectives, puzzlements, and intuitions are not merely "out there," aspects of an abstract understanding that can be kept at a distance from one's own commitments and identity. A liberally educated person makes learning and understanding, confusion and contradiction part of themselves, of their identity and quest for meaning. Learning is incorporated into the person's sense of self and construction of personal meaning. Thus the elements of a liberal education participate actively in the processes of *formation* that define each of our students and ourselves as a person of faith, as an American citizen in a democratic society, and as a responsible member of the global community.

In the title for this essay, I refer to liberal education as both opportunity and challenge for the faith-based university. I believe that the kind of student most likely to attend a Christian college is already someone disposed to read carefully, deeply, analytically, and reverentially, like the young Messiah graduate who met me at the airport. They already are imbued with what I might call "the hermeneutic imperative." This is a discipline whose importance extends far beyond the reading of biblical text. Whether history or mathematics, philosophy or Shakespeare, the text of DNA strands, a Renaissance painting, or the paths of planets in their orbits, the college student's first challenge is to read and listen carefully, patiently, and sympathetically, yet critically. A young person who has grown up studying sacred texts has begun to develop precisely those dispositions, and they should transfer successfully to all the texts of liberal learning if students and faculty approach such texts in an appropriate manner.

Moreover, someone raised as a member of a faith community has probably also developed elements of what the Lilly Endowment's Craig Dykstra has dubbed "the pastoral imagination." This is a term we learned as we prepared to embark on our four-year study of the education of clergy in Protestant, Catholic, and Jewish seminaries.[4] The pastoral imagination is a habit of mind in which well-prepared clergy who are readers of sacred texts have developed the capacity to connect interpretations, nuances, or ways of making sense of those texts to the variety of contexts, from the personal to the political, in which congregants or protagonists dwell. Thus the pastor, priest, or rabbi regularly confronts the challenge of connecting the enduring contents of holy texts with the constantly shifting panorama of events in the world. These connections constitute the contents of a weekly sermon, a eulogy for a stricken community member, the dedication of a building, or the individual counseling offered to a congregant who has been stricken by illness or confronts a crisis of faith.

In the work of members of the clergy, the pastoral imagination describes the itinerary that carries the scholarly pastor from hermeneutic to homiletic, from understanding the deep and multiple meanings of scripture and relating them to the ever-changing challenges of life and death in the larger world. Yet this interpretive movement is not limited to religious leaders. The challenge of liberal learning in general is to help our students deeply understand the ideas of both sacred texts and the texts of the humanities, sciences, social sciences, mathematics, and other aspects of worldly wisdom so that they can plumb their depths in ways that make those insights available and usable to guide their lives in the world. Whether in a religious tradition or in a secular one, we also strive to connect those ideas to the responsibilities of living a moral, ethical, and generous life compatible with the principles of a good and democratic society.

If exercise of a version of the pastoral imagination is a goal of liberal education in a faith-based university, we cannot ignore the centrality of the second principle, the principle of multiple perspectives, of plural interpretations, of *machloket* as a necessary condition of and prerequisite to the *shalom* of full, rich understanding and thus of a deeper sense of personal meaning and identity. That principle of multiple perspectives will often be the stumbling block for the program of a faith-based institution.

While John Dewey described the impulse that animates the typical human thinker as a "quest for certainty," I believe that when we as educators take on the responsibility of teaching students to profess both their understanding and their faith, we assume responsibility for teaching them to resist those instincts that encourage taking the shortcuts to certainty, even though at times faith may encourage such paths. Instead, as liberal educators we are obligated to lead our students to engage in a "quest for uncertainty." Although the prophet Isaiah praises God for making the rough places smooth and exalting the valleys, the pedagogies of liberal learning must not pursue that path. A liberal education teaches students, contrary to Isaiah's vision, to make the smooth places rough before they can be trusted to be smooth again. Before the liberally educated student can make a deep commitment unilaterally, she must appreciate the inherent complexity, richness, nuance, and ambiguity of texts and their messages. To the extent that a liberally educated person has achieved a modicum of certainty, it is only because he has taken on and negotiated the potholes and rough places, not avoided them.

To this point I have argued for the interplay of educating for both depth and a plural view as the requirements for deep understanding and personal meaning. An important challenge to this claim, however, is to ask whether these are merely hypothetical imaginings on my part and whether there is any empirical evidence that well-educated men or women of faith indeed think and act in these ways, and if so, what that kind of thinking looks like. Unless we can offer somewhat more operational and behavioral accounts of such learning, the likelihood of being able to design educational experiences to engender such learning is rather low.

An Empirical Study: Epistemic Switching

I now turn our attention at some length to a new psychological study examining how scholars of faith and scholars who are secular read and make sense of biblical texts and their interpretations that reflect clear tensions and contradictions between the perspective of faith and the perspective of disciplinary—in this case historical—understanding. This study, published in *The Journal of Learning Sciences* as "Between *Veritas* and *Communitas*: Epistemic Switching in the Reading of Academic and Sacred History," was conducted by the psychologists Eli Gottlieb of Jerusalem's Mandel Leadership Institute and Sam Wineburg of the Stanford University School of Education.[5] This is a long, rich, and quite detailed study, and I cannot do justice to its wealth of ideas and empirical observations. Nevertheless, my reading of the work in a much earlier draft was largely responsible for inspiring the ideas I develop in this essay. For this I am grateful to Gottlieb and Wineburg, though at times I may interpret their findings and extrapolate their implications far beyond the authors' quite responsible comfort zones.

The authors were interested in discovering how individuals who were simultaneously members of both a faith community and a disciplinary community of scholars negotiated the tensions created when responding to texts that challenged the norms of one or another of their two identities and affiliations. More specifically, they designed an investigation to study how religiously committed historians interpreted texts where religious traditions and disciplinary modes of thinking were in conflict. In this particular case, they asked a number of historians to read biblical texts describing the exodus of the Israelites from Egypt in conjunction with critical archaeological and historical texts that raised serious questions about the historicity of the biblical accounts. For the purposes of this chapter, I shall only attend to the responses of two of their participants, Professor B, a Christian historian, and Professor C, a Jewish historian.

I shall take the liberty of quoting extensively both from the historians whose thinking they tapped in their investigation and from the analyses that Gottlieb and Wineburg offered to explain and extend their findings. My purpose is to treat the thinking of these historians as instances of how mature scholars can engage with their subjects both critically and devotionally, the strategies and dispositions they have developed to participate with integrity in both their communities, and the lessons we can draw as educators about how to prepare our own students to perform similar feats of both intelligence and identity.

Listen to the voice of Professor B, the Christian historian, as he ponders the contradictions between the biblical narrative in Exodus and archaeological accounts that report no physical evidence of the movements of a mass of over 600,000 persons from Egypt, across a miraculously divided Sea of Reeds, to a mountain in Sinai and then around that arid region for forty years, during which all the adults who fled Egypt ostensibly die.

> The ways in which the faithful assume on the one hand that that which is described in Scripture is equivalent to historical

narrative seems simplistic. But equally simplistic to me are interpretive stances by scholars that assume that if no record exists, save this initially oral, ultimately written tradition, then clearly we have a case of a tradition that is mythical in the sense of being fictional.... I prefer, as they say, *a hermeneutic of reserved judgment rather than a hermeneutic of suspicion.*

Gottlieb and Wineburg comment on those observations:

> Professor B's "hermeneutic of reserved judgment" functioned as the balance point between religious faith and the desire for evidence. On one hand, he refused to reject a claim because of lack of evidence. On the other, faith did not trump the historical project of carefully sifting through and evaluating evidence. He explained: "All of that is part of me ... [historian and believer] are not contradictory, they are not compartmentalized. They are supplemental in a sometimes mysterious way ... I can't not be a historian when I think about matters of faith and the narratives of the tradition. But then, I can't not be a Christian when I do historical scholarship."

While Professor B appeared to employ a heuristic of simultaneity as he pondered the challenge posed by the Exodus texts, Professor C responded somewhat differently when asked how he would deal with the complexities of the texts. "On what day of the week? When I'm teaching my class or when I'm in the synagogue?" Gottlieb and Wineburg observe that "Professor C's response brought into focus the choice of guilds before him: should he affiliate at that moment with the guild of professional historians he joins every Monday morning at the university or the body of co-religionists who engage with these texts quite differently in synagogue on Saturday morning?

He elaborated:

> When I'm teaching my courses I'm bound by the rules of historical research and I have an obligation to explain to my students what the tradition of historical scholarship has to say about this material.... Now when I'm in a synagogue, I'm not going to be talking about the historical evidence of the Exodus, I'm going to be ... —contemporizing, metaphorizing, allegorizing—because essentially my task there is to make the traditional come alive and address people where they live. To do that, as I said, the historical veracity of the business is hardly relevant at all.

Maturity is about understanding the value of the past as represented in tradition because, really, people don't live and die as historians, they live and die as people (laughter)... [People] need nourishment from the past; they need people around them who share common ideas and ideals, and an ethos and a moral framework. And historical reasoning, when it's directed at penetrating mythic ideas, is designed to free people from that. But once they're free from it, what are they going to fall into? Usually some kind of ideology or another, which is equally specious, like nationalism or socialism or fascism, whatever *ism* is around. That's what replaces the debunked religious myth. All of those *isms*, although claiming to be scientific, appeal to science as a mythic reality rather than as an empirical tool.

I am drawing upon only a small slice of the rich body of interviews and reflections of the scholars who were studied by Gottlieb and Wineburg, and similarly only scratching the surface of their subtle and inventive analysis. Yet what we see is instructive. The challenge of negotiating between their faith commitments and their disciplinary norms appears to have made their thinking more subtle and layered rather than bifurcated and simplified. There is a sophistication that grows from looking at an important part of one's experience from multiple perspectives yet having to integrate those perspectives into one identity and one sense of self. What might we learn about the education of young scholars from this examination of the thinking of more mature ones?[26]

Gottlieb and Wineburg offer a particularly insightful interpretation of the findings they have reported, in which they introduce the concept that organizes their entire enterprise, *epistemic switching*. In this article destined to become a classic of both the cognitive and learning sciences as well as the intersection of studies of religion and of human behavior, they observe:

> To recapitulate: we found that historians, religious or not, tended to do what historians do: they placed documents into broader contexts and drew on conceptual categories like anachronism to characterize how the present plays fast and loose with the past....
>
> Yet, when it came to the Exodus task, our block of eight historians split into two camps—those with and without religious commitments. When the non-religious encountered claims that

appealed to a religious sensibility (either deriving from Scripture or the ancillary documents), they hoisted a disciplinary red card, crying foul at rogue logic or dismissing these claims as simply "not history." Religious historians, on the other hand, openly acknowledged alternative logics and tried to navigate between the dictates of their professional training and their reverence for sacred history. They did this by engaging in *epistemic switching*, varying their criteria for truth, reliability, and warrant according to the associations and allegiances that a given text triggered. Some engaged both logics simultaneously, reading texts with a kind of epistemological bifocality, as did Professor B; others, like Professor C, treated the logics as separate and equal, always using one or the other but never both at the same time....

We sat people down in a single space and gave them texts from different worlds. Their only movement *per se* was to shift in their chairs or reach for their reading glasses. Confronting texts that made different demands on their affiliations and commitments, they neither became different people nor renounced membership in one community to take up residence in another. Rather, they engaged in *mental* switches, nimbly shifting between epistemological frames that reflected multiple and distinct ways of engaging the past. The importance of our work lies in documenting the fluidity of these switches, a seamlessness that expands and complicates our notions of human functioning. People express their multiplicity even without changing clothes or putting on different hats. Indeed, the very spheres that philosophers claim must move in separate conceptual orbits ... not only come together with finesse as real people sit down and read texts about the sacred past, but may act in mutually corrective ways that stretch our understanding of the human capacity for complexity and nuance.

We use the term *epistemic switching* to describe how participants dealt with the multiple memberships evoked by these texts. This term denotes a participant's use of multiple epistemic frames (e.g., historical, theological, scientific) for interpreting documentary evidence. We prefer the term "epistemic switching" to "membership switching" because when such switches occurred, they typically involved more than a shift from one self-description to another. They generally signaled a shift from one set of assumptions about the nature of knowledge to another.

The concept of "epistemic switching" is a lovely way of characterizing the cognitive complexity exhibited by the two historians. I am impressed by the "think-alouds" of the two "believers." I am struck by the richness, the nuance, the flexibility, and the generosity of spirit of their thought. Moreover, their epistemologies are not only ways of thinking and knowing. They are intimately tied to the historians' identities, to their sense of who they are and who they must become. Thus, in terms of the three principles of a liberal education, these historians not only exhibit the virtues of hermeneutic skill and the power of multiple perspectives; they also exemplify the connection between these and the development of personal meaning and the formation of identity.

Those modes of thinking are reflections of what a deep liberal education ought to look like, and the context of a faith-based liberal arts research university is an ideal setting for nurturing just that kind of human being and citizen, and the habits of mind, of practice, and of heart that are to be developed. Nevertheless, as an educator I am not satisfied with "epistemic switching" as an educational goal, even if it is a powerful description of the adaptive behavior observed by the two historians. There is an aspect of that capacity that strikes me as somewhat too passive or reactive. I believe that as liberal educators we should attempt to go beyond the capacity to adapt and switch when confronted with a problematic intellectual challenge. A liberal education should provide students with the disposition to anticipate, resonate with, and even seek out contrasting and dissenting ideas from others as a positive feature of valued discourse and not only as a safe haven when the going gets tough. We should help students treat *machloket* as a source of growth and as a crucible for testing and nurturing the values of both faith and democratic engagement. And the only way they can learn these things is if we provide them with repeated opportunities to practice, rehearse, stumble, and ultimately internalize them.

I would therefore propose that we explicitly aim to exemplify, encourage, and directly instruct students in the development of *epistemic empathy* and *epistemic mindfulness* as modes of thought and action. Our students should not only be tolerant of multiple, challenging interpretations; they should also be capable of generating them, inviting them, and employing them intentionally and even joyfully in their studies, in their relationships, and in their work.

PEDAGOGICAL CHALLENGES

The path that we have set upon is ambitious and daunting. It is not enough to declare the virtue of epistemic mindfulness; it must be intentionally taught and learned, modeled and challenged, practiced and performed. We are not speaking of a set of skills or competencies that can be merely stated, assigned as readings or exercises, and then tested for mastery. Nor can such learning be located in an elective silo, Epistemic Mindfulness 101. If these habits of mind, hand, and heart are to be learned well, they must permeate the undergraduate curriculum whether what is learned is theology or sociology, American history or evolutionary biology. We are describing the formation of identity, both personal and professional, communal and civic. It is a goal for liberal education in a democratic society that takes both its faith and its democracy seriously. The formation of identity rests on the underlying development of ways of thinking, judging, and feeling that constitute challenging goals for any educational effort. If we needed any reminder of how elusive and difficult are the skills of epistemic empathy, flexibility, and mindfulness, we need only listen to the discourse of our political leaders during an election year, and the extent to which they are typically deaf and blind to the rays of insight and wisdom in the views of their opponents, whether on the left or the right.

In the professions like law, medicine, nursing, teaching, engineering, and the clergy, the importance of intentional pedagogies is well understood. These fields have developed "signature pedagogies" that afford their future practitioners ample opportunities to observe, analyze, unpack, practice, and critique their accomplishment of those demanding professional practices. It is no accident that pedagogical practices like rounds and rotations in nursing and medicine, studio design practica in engineering and architecture, repeated practice of hermeneutics and homiletics in clergy education, the ubiquitous practices of Socratic dialogue across law school classes, all represent signature pedagogies for those professions. They permeate the curriculum, toward the end of the program, in most of the clinical fields like nursing, engineering, and medicine, and toward the beginning of programs in American law schools. These signature pedagogies may look quite different from one profession to another, but they share a set of underlying principles that have been articulated by my Carnegie Foundation colleague Anne Colby as *enactment, dailiness,* and *embodiment.*

The principle of *enactment* describes the observation that in most of these types of teaching and learning the students are active, engaged, highly visible, and therefore personally accountable for their learning on a regular basis. They are not passively sitting in lectures or other traditional classroom activities. The principle of *dailiness* describes the extent to which the teaching practices are repeated again and again, day after day, month after month. If you intend to develop new habits, be they of thinking or performing, there is a need for repetition, rehearsal, and continuous modeling and feedback. Habits are not the product of doing something really well once. Finally, both teachers and students must *embody* those practices and ideas. The formation of identity results from the combination of modeling, peer culture, and the active "trying on" of alternative versions of oneself, called in some quarters "identity drafts." Moreover, because this kind of learning is not superficial but cuts close to the bone of one's sense of self, the process can become tense and uncomfortable and students may well push back and resist the invasion of their personal and intellectual space. That will be a sign that the pedagogy is indeed reaching its mark.

A particular challenge in a faith-based university may well be the more limited presence in one's learning environment of multiple role models, exhibiting a range of modes of thinking and being, that create occasions for trying on "identity drafts." When there are legitimate reasons for insisting on a homogeneity of ideology and faith commitments among students and faculty members, the obligation to create a positive atmosphere of *machloket* will require creative development of pedagogical options, whether through visitors, technological communications and representations, case studies, or the insistence that in all possible situations of learning faculty members and students ask themselves, "How might it be otherwise?"

Since the kinds of pedagogy I have described are so highly interactive and challenging, they are also far more uncertain than the more conventional modes of teaching like lectures and demonstrations. When a university commits itself to deep liberal education that incorporates the delicate balance and interaction between faith and questioning, the devotional and the critical, it cannot take for granted that what it intends for students to learn and become will be achieved. (Truth be told, one cannot take such things for granted even when the teaching is utterly conventional and didactic!) The work of teaching and learning, therefore, will need to be accompanied by an ongoing *scholarship of teaching and learning*, wherein the experiences of learning are carefully documented and the impact of education is investigated in both the long and the short term. I shall develop this idea more fully in the closing section.

The Institutional Challenge

What then is the role of the university itself in this endeavor? I offer you three challenges if you are to address the difficulties and take advantage of the opportunities presented to you as a faith-based liberal arts university. These are the challenges of *intentionality, complexity*, and *inquiry*.

First, the university must face the challenges of developing an institution-wide intentionality with regard to teaching and learning, one that permeates its culture in the same way that Baylor's faith commitment permeates its culture. Second, the university must come to terms with the need to complicate, challenge, and confront the beliefs and lives of its students and itself. This is pedagogy of *machloket*, a pedagogy that fosters a more complex and ambiguous world that students must strain to make their own. Third, the leaders and faculty members of the university must recognize that these pedagogies of analytic reading and thinking, of multiple perspectives and ways of thinking, and of personal meaning and formation are highly complex, demanding, and above all, uncertain. As they are pedagogies of uncertainty, they demand of us as professional educators that we treat our efforts as grand and courageous experiments whose consequences for our students and ourselves must be subjected to careful documentation and research so we can truly take responsibility for their consequences.

Intentionality manifests itself as faculty express their commitments to develop a shared sense of the liberal learning expected of students, and make clear to the students that this is a shared responsibility, one that the faculty cannot do alone. Students will need to take responsibility for meeting their teachers halfway in this journey. Students are not necessarily ready for this kind of teaching. Prepare them for its discomforts, help them prepare to feel resistant and uncomfortable, anticipate their emotions and join them in acknowledging and celebrating them.

Recognize that you are, as I noted earlier, acting against the grain of Isaiah's prophecy: You are not here to make the rough places smooth, to fill in the valleys and level the mountains. You are here to make the smooth places rough, to recognize that there are valleys and mountains that confront the educated person of faith in a democracy, and that the responsibility of Baylor's teachers and students is to invite and welcome this roughness as the crucible in which their intelligence, their faith, and their civic responsibilities in a free and equal society must be developed and mature.

Institutional intentionality is not easily accomplished in academic environments long dominated by notions of academic freedom wherein each faculty member does what he or she pleases. Yet in our professional schools we have long recognized that the need to train future professionals to serve the greater society responsibly trumps many aspects of individual faculty academic freedom.

But do we corrupt undergraduate liberal education by arguing that it should become more similar to professional education? I think not. The purpose of a liberal education is learning to profess. The purpose of a liberal education is to develop the habits of mind, the habits of practice, and the habits of the heart needed to function effectively as a citizen in a democracy, as a responsible and devoted member of a faith community, and as a member of a family and personal community to which one is devoted. We profess our intelligence, our skills, and our sensibilities. We profess our faith, our love, our doubts, and our questions.

We therefore seek an intentional pedagogy of evangelical liberal education with the development of epistemic empathy and mindfulness at its core. And to this end, faculty members at a Christian research university must take responsibility for rendering this kind of teaching and learning as a question of scholarship, a scholarship of teaching and learning. To the extent that we seek to educate the hearts and minds of our students, we are invading their private spaces as much as do psychotherapists and surgeons. We hold members of those professions responsible to investigate carefully whether their treatments are efficacious and their interventions are salutary. Why should we as educators hold ourselves any less accountable?[7]

I conclude as I began, with reference to my alma mater the University of Chicago. The University of Chicago was established by John D. Rockefeller as a Baptist institution, and its first president, William Rainey Harper, was a distinguished Bible scholar, one of whose first jobs was teaching Hebrew at Chicago's Baptist Union Theological Seminary. (Since my first job was also teaching Hebrew, I always identified with Mr. Harper!) Harper died tragically of cancer at the age of 49, completing his commentary on the Book of Joel on his deathbed. Harper was a real pioneer in imagining the idea of a research university. He argued that a university ought to be an institution for which no problem, topic, or issue was off limits to inquiry. Faculty members and students should be encouraged to treat everything around them as proper material for investigation.

That being the case, Harper also insisted that the institution of the research university itself should always be an ongoing educational experiment, and as such, it should always be investigating its own efforts and their impact on students and on the community surrounding the institution. I have argued in this paper that the faith-based research university that is committed to liberal learning as a central element of its mission must recognize the extent to which it is also an ongoing experiment. Harper's admonition applies as fittingly to Baylor as it did to Chicago. Liberal learning will only be an opportunity as well as a challenge if it can be pursued in ways that will help the university learn from its own efforts and transfer that learning to the improvement of its educational mission.

6

THE BIBLE, BAPTISTS, AND THE CHALLENGE OF CHRISTIAN HIGHER EDUCATION

— *Mark Noll* —

Francis A. McAnaney Professor of History, University of Notre Dame

I am honored to present this address. My personal knowledge extends to only a few of the contributions that Baylor University has made over its long history to the intellectual life of Baptist communities in Texas and that in more recent years it has offered far beyond Texas and far beyond Baptists to a much broader range of academic enterprises and a much wider circle of Christian believers. But even that partial knowledge leaves me impressed and grateful for what the university and its personnel have accomplished. In a quick perusal of the website, I was surprised to see how many notable contributors I recognized in Baylor's departments of English, history, law, music, philosophy, religion, and Spanish, and in the Honors College and Truett Seminary. I did not recognize names in engineering, computing, or the sciences, but I certainly know of outstanding achievements coming from those sectors as well. In the hard drive of my computer there is stored a short paragraph on Baylor that I have used recently in several published works; I am delighted to repeat another version of that paragraph here: "Christian higher education has been given a special boost in recent years by remarkable developments at Baylor University. With 2012 now at hand, it is clear that Baylor's grandest original goals in the 2012 program have not been fully accomplished, but it is also clear that those efforts are continuing and that they constitute absolutely the most ambitious, far-reaching, and comprehensive institutional attempt in recent American history to do the proper Christian thing for the life of the mind."

Baylor University, in other words, stands as an unusually fine example of what an institution of higher learning rooted in the Baptist tradition can accomplish in a contemporary intellectual environment that undervalues undergraduate teaching, that dismisses Texas as the blowhard part of the country, that takes little interest in Baptist history, and that has almost no desire to learn what a Baptist perspective can contribute to the worlds of learning.

I mean this tribute to Baylor and its achievements sincerely. But for a historian to examine "The Bible, Baptists, and the Challenge of Christian Higher Education" is immediately to confront two conclusions. The first is that the place of Scripture poses a real problem in the modern Christian university. The second is that Baptists have contributed a great deal to creating that problem. This address explores briefly why I think there is a real problem respecting the Bible in the modern Christian university. It then moves to reviewing main points of generally Protestant and specifically Baptist history in order to explain why I think Baptist approaches to Scripture have both greatly helped and greatly hindered the purposes of Christian higher education.[1]

* * *

The place of Scripture in the modern Christian university is a problem because Christian intellectual life in the contemporary western world requires an exercise in tightrope walking. The wire is strung between faithful devotion to divine revelation and responsible engagement with modern learning. It is much easier to fall off this wire than to maintain your balance.

In the current American scene we have several obvious examples of falling off the wire into a crass biblicism that disregards the legitimate benefits of simply taking a humble place in modern intellectual life. The most obvious example of this destructive biblicism is creation science, where a determined practice of nineteenth-century literal biblical hermeneutics and dedicated commitment to persuasion by adversarial populism overwhelms the critically constructed "best results" of worthy scientific work. But there are other examples in which zealous adherents to Scripture simply toss out the baby of well-grounded learning with the bathwater of learning abused for God-denying purposes. These examples include manic single-issue public advocacy that claims to represent "biblical politics"; runaway Americanism that depicts our nation's early history as the land of the converted and the home of the true-blue evangelical; and the cruder forms of "intelligent design" that repeat William Paley's error of using God to fill in the gaps of contemporary scientific knowledge.

The common mistake of those falling off the wire in this direction is to neglect central teachings of the Scriptures themselves. If God made all humans in his image, if the ability to learn about the external world is a gift given by God to all those made in his image, if Scripture teaches that believers in God are also susceptible to error, and if Scripture testifies repeatedly that all people have a significant capacity for genuine insight on some aspects of human affairs—then Bible believers should be the first to expect genuine intellectual insights from the entire human community, especially in the study of the material world, mathematics, and those aspects of experience that do not deal explicitly with humans standing directly before God.

These problems are more obvious where the *Christian* element predominates when examining the modern Christian university. A different set of problems appears frequently where the *modern* or the *university* elements predominate. Falling off the wire on that side means simply receiving elite opinion in any academic specialty with no effort to assess that opinion through Christian beliefs rooted in Scripture. A few specific examples will be mentioned later, but for now it is enough to recognize the common mistake in this way of falling off the high wire. That common mistake is to relegate Christian belief to a private space that never intersects meaningfully with the public spaces where learning takes place.

* * *

If this brief account of problems about the Bible in the modern university is anywhere near accurate, why do Baptists share responsibility for the problems besetting Christian universities today as they set about their tasks? The following paragraphs limit consideration to

Protestant institutions, but for those institutions the place to begin is at the beginning of Protestantism itself. My brief overview of early Protestant history emphasizes those features that Baptists value the most.

The furor over Martin Luther's *Ninety-Five Theses* of 1517 is properly regarded as the flash point that instigated the Protestant Reformation. In light of later Protestant insistence on Scripture as the defining norm for doctrine and life, it is noteworthy, however, that the *Ninety-Five Theses* contained very little direct appeal to the Bible as such. Instead, the theses mostly took up questions about the theology and practice of indulgences.

When, however, Luther's Latin proposal for an in-house academic debate was translated into German and republished by several enterprising printers, it is well known that a large populace responded with enthusiasm even as the pope and his associates responded with outrage. The ensuing controversy witnessed an almost immediate explosion of print, which in turn led to an almost immediate shift in the controversy's center of gravity.

Specific questions about Christian doctrine certainly remained important, but almost immediately they were joined and frequently superseded by questions concerning Christian authority: how could faithful believers know what was true, and who could guide them in finding out? The *Ninety-Five Theses* were posted on October 31, 1517; less than a year later Luther was called from his own town of Wittenberg to meet a representative of the pope, Cardinal Thomas Cajetan, in the imperial city of Augsburg. At Augsburg the controversy over the doctrine and practice of indulgences almost instantly expanded into controversy over the use and authority of Scripture. Luther wanted to cite the Bible to defend his positions, but Cajetan never took this bait; he insisted instead that Luther had to return to the established teachings of the church.

Since the spheres of religion and society were so intimately conjoined in early modern Europe, Luther's challenge to religious authority was quickly perceived as a challenge to authority in general. That broader challenge was apparent when Luther traveled in April 1521 to an imperial Diet convened by the Holy Roman Emperor, Charles V. Although Charles lacked experience as emperor and everything spoken in German had to be translated for him into Latin, he nonetheless represented at Worms the personal embodiment of Christendom. Christendom was the ideal built up over the previous seven centuries that the interests of religion and society could be harmonized into one completely integrated whole. Before such an august personage representing such a well-established ideal, Martin Luther appeared as a solitary monk who in his private spiritual journey had become convinced that Scripture taught much that the pope, the emperor, and all Christendom had tragically misconstrued.

When Luther came before the imperial court, he said he would recant what he had written, but only upon one condition. That condition amounted to a quintessentially Protestant challenge: "Therefore, I ask by the mercy of God, may your most serene majesty, most illustrious lordships, or anyone at all who is able, either high or low, bear witness, expose my errors, *overthrowing them by the writings of the prophets and the evangelists*."[2]

But that statement did not satisfy the Emperor, who asked Luther to say more. In response came Luther's famous words: "Since then your serene majesty and your lordships seek a simple answer, I will give it . . . : Unless I am convinced by the testimony of the Scriptures or by clear reason (for I do not trust either in the pope or in councils alone, since it is well known that they have often erred and contradicted themselves), *I am bound by the Scriptures I have quoted and my conscience is captive to the Word of God*. I cannot and I will not retract anything, since it is neither safe nor right to go against conscience."[3]

This dramatic statement in this most auspicious setting defined a baseline for all later Protestants and especially for Baptists: they would follow the Bible before all other authorities—even when, as many Baptists later concluded, the Bible taught truths at considerable variance from what Luther found in Scripture. The statement also defined a second landmark that has been crucial for Baptist development from the moment Baptists existed: "my conscience," or the individual Bible reader aware of standing before the face of God, would be the final guide for interpreting the supremely authoritative Scripture.

But potential problems for this combination of Bible plus conscience were apparent from the start. Immediately after Luther had finished speaking his piece, the emperor's spokesman called him to account for setting himself up as superior to the great councils of the Catholic church that had already ruled on many of the issues he was addressing. "In this," the imperial secretary told Luther, "you are completely mad." Then he went on with words that forecast any number of problems in the later history of Protestant university life: "For what purpose does it serve to raise a new dispute about matters condemned through so many centuries by church and council? Unless perhaps a reason must be given to just anyone about anything whatsoever. But if it were granted that whoever contradicts the councils and the common understanding of the church must be overcome by Scripture passages, we will have nothing in Christianity that is certain or decided."[4]

What the spokesman saw perceptively was that conscience alone plus Scripture alone had the potential for incessant intellectual instability. Yet by the time that the emperor and the pope's representatives figured out what they wanted to do with Luther, he had long since left Worms. Luther's prince, the Elector Frederick of Saxony, was torn between a desire to protect the theologian who was bringing renown to his land and the need to show deference to the emperor. Frederick's creative response was to maintain a public position of noncommittal impartiality while arranging, under strictest secrecy, for Luther to be "kidnapped" and spirited away to a secret retreat, the Castle Wartburg near Eisenach.

As soon as Luther was settled in the Wartburg, he turned his great energy to preparing a German-language translation of the New Testament. The result in only a few short months was Luther's 1522 German New Testament. It was immediately noteworthy for the chance it gave Luther to accentuate the themes of Scripture that most directly fueled his reforming fire. A much-noticed instance was his translation of a key passage about faith and justification found toward the end of the third chapter of Paul's Epistle to the Romans. Luther added the word "alone" to the Apostle's statement that believers are "justified without the works of the law by faith."

A second noteworthy feature of Luther's first momentously important New Testament was its annotations, which came in two forms. In slender margins alongside the translated text of Scripture, Luther inserted quotations from what he considered pertinent Old

Testament texts and also explained what he felt the New Testament authors were trying to say. He also supplied prefaces, first to the New Testament as a whole and then to each of the individual books.

In the general preface to the entire New Testament Luther told why there needed to be a preface at all. His very first sentences explained that "it would be right and proper for this book to go forth without any prefaces or extraneous names attached and simply have its own say under its own name." Yet Luther did provide an introductory preface because "many unfounded interpretations . . . have scattered the thought of Christians to a point where no one any longer knows what is gospel or law, New Testament or Old." It was, therefore, a "necessity" for Luther to give some "notice . . . by which the ordinary man can be rescued from his former delusions, set on the right track, and taught what he is to look for in this book, so that he may not seek laws and commandments where he ought to be seeking the gospel and promises of God."5

This very first Protestant Bible translation mingled the ideal and the real as they would be consistently mingled in Protestant history, and nowhere more thoroughly than in American experience. The ideal was biblical authority alone; the real was constant effort by those with authority to make sure that others were carefully guided so that they could grasp what "the Bible alone" really meant.

One more incident in Luther's early reforming career is pertinent. While Luther was hidden away in the Wartburg Castle, colleagues who shared his desire for reform got to work in Wittenberg. They were led by an older university professor and cleric, Andreas Bodenstein von Karlstadt, who believed that a right interpretation of Scripture demanded more and faster changes than Luther had ever desired. In short order Karlstadt drastically simplified the ritual of the Mass, led the destruction of artistic images in Wittenberg churches, and took many other radical steps. Luther and the Elector Frederick were furious. To check what they saw not as reform but a rush into chaos, Frederick called Luther back to Wittenberg to deliver a series of sermons during Lent. And then Frederick, with Luther's full backing, banished Karlstadt from Saxony because Karlstadt's interpretations of Scripture seemed so dangerous to both the Elector Frederick and the theologian Luther. This incident is particularly relevant to

Baptist history because Baptists would long stand with Karlstadt and protest against heavy-handed authority that constrained free exercise in following free interpretations of Scripture.

So here is how things stood with the Bible before the Protestant Reformation was even ten years old. Scripture, as God's written revelation that could nonetheless be corrupted by self-seeking church officials, was the supreme authority for all of life's important questions. Moreover, the individual standing humbly before God could follow his own conscience (and, quite a bit later, her own conscience) in grasping the message of Scripture. In turn, that clear perception could purify Christian teaching, reform church corruption, and bring new life in the Holy Spirit to individuals and Christian communities alike.

But, of course, that is not all. Since few could read the Bible's original Greek and Hebrew for themselves, it was necessary for translations to be prepared so that people could read Scripture in vernacular languages. But wherever translation takes place, the labors of the translators shade the final product. For Scripture, a translated text is no longer "the Bible alone."

And there is more. As soon as there was a Protestant movement appealing to Scripture as ultimate authority, there were Protestant *movements* differing on how best to interpret the supremely authoritative Scripture. Some of those differences were minor, while others were literally deadly in the effect they had on those who maintained them. And so began the Protestant swinging to and fro that has gone on since late in 1517 to this day: strong assertions of conscience captive to the Word of God are pulled back by authoritative directives from religious or intellectual or political leaders about what one's conscience is supposed to find when it opens the Scriptures.

For the long-term future of higher education, what Baptists did with the baseline Protestant commitment to both Scripture and the individual conscience had momentous consequences. Two solid recent books on the history of Baptists worldwide show how Protestantism took a particularly significant turn when Baptists emerged on the scene. One is Robert E. Johnson's *A Global Introduction to Baptist Churches*, and the other is David Bebbington's *Baptists through the Centuries*.[6] Both authors do a fine job of making Baptist history comprehensible. In addition, however, they also show how the great potential contribution of Baptists to modern higher education has been matched by significant problems that Baptist traditions create for university life.

Johnson and Bebbington detail clearly that Baptists were offshoots of the English Puritan movements that insisted on *scriptura sola* as the sole reliable basis for faithful Christianity and the most effective source for correcting the halfway reform of the national Church of England. From that earliest history, a very high view of biblical authority has remained central to almost all later Baptist movements. Yet even more distinctly Baptist has been the way that this loyalty to Scripture is practiced. Baptists pushed the logic of "the priesthood of all believers" beyond where most of their fellow Protestants wanted to go. In the Baptist view, a properly functioning Christianity required not just diligence in following Scripture, but the personal and intentional commitment of each church member to practice that diligence. For Baptists, common Protestant teaching about the lordship or kingship of Christ was taken to mean that no intermediate authority should stand between God and the gathering of his people to worship and serve him.

Movement from a desire for more thorough reform to the creation of distinctly Baptist churches occurred early in the seventeenth century. Dissenters who had already separated from the national church and fled to Holland in order to find greater religious freedom provided the spark. In 1609 John Smyth, a Cambridge-trained Separate, baptized himself and a few others and so created the first Baptist church. Smyth himself remained only briefly with the Baptist congregation he established before moving on in a further quest for true religion. More stable leaders, like Thomas Helwys, provided continuity of leadership and also brought Baptist principles back to England where the movement gradually spread.

These earliest Baptists were "General" because they believed in the potential efficacy of Christ's death for all humans. In theological terms, they were Arminians who stressed the freedom of the human will. Before long, however, they were joined by "Particular" Baptists who maintained the era's standard Calvinist teaching that Christ died particularly for the elect rather than for humanity as a whole.

Within a generation from their founding, both "Generals" and "Particulars" would begin baptizing by immersion, the standard practice that distinguishes Baptist churches around the world to this day. Baptists soon developed extensive arguments drawn from "the Bible alone" to defend the practice of adult baptism by immersion upon personal profession of faith. Yet this approach to baptism represented even more a protest against the Christendom idea of inherited or bestowed Christian identification that the traditional practice of infant baptism symbolized. To be a follower of Christ meant to commit oneself personally rather than to rely on the mediation of family, church, or a supposedly Christian society. The broad preconviction underlying this specific baptismal practice was a positive vision of the self's individual responsibility under God and a negative vision of human institutions or traditions as distorting that personal relationship.

In turn, this combination of positive and negative commitments gave birth to the principles that have ever since resounded through Baptist history: "religious freedom," "the right of private judgment," "soul competency," and a "gathered church." A moving recapitulation of those commitments was offered in 1861 by Johann Gerhard Oncken, the great pioneer of Baptist life in Germany, when he stood before a monument to Martin Luther in the same city of Worms where Luther had made his famous protest to the Emperor Charles V: "I rejoiced to think that the spirit of Martin Luther can never be quite extinguished while the Word of God, which he gave us in our native tongue, shall exist. Yes, we Baptists owe him our best treasure and we shall do well ever to keep before us Luther's heroic example of nonsubmission to worldly power in matters of religion."[7]

For Christian higher education, especially higher education at a Protestant university, this Baptist anchorage in Scripture has made a positive and fundamental contribution. The 1925 Faith and Message Statement of the Southern Baptist Convention has often been quoted for how it defined Scripture: "it has God for its author, salvation for its end, and truth, without any mixture of error, for its matter." It has been less often quoted for what the statement claims about the extent of biblical authority: "the principles by which God will judge us . . . the true center of Christian union, and the supreme standard by which all human conduct, creeds and religious opinions should be tried."[8] But these last phrases are the ones that suggest the imperative importance of Scripture for human learning: because the Bible offers an infallible message of salvation, it offers as well a fruitful guide to everything that human beings do and believe—in other words, to the subjects that constitute the curriculum of a modern university.

The great gift of the Baptist tradition to higher education is the constant reminder that without Scripture, personally applied, there is no Christian foundation upon which to construct the edifice of learning. To expand upon the insight of J. G. Oncken, Baptist anchorage in Scripture provides the resources for "non-submission to worldly powers" in academic life generally and not just in "matters of religion" specifically.

As any academic with even the slightest self-awareness recognizes, the force of "worldly powers"—or widely accepted conventions—in academic life can be all but overwhelming. For example, if conventions of scientific practice do not allow a consideration of teleology, it is very difficult for individual Christian scholars to consider nature under the aegis of divine providence. When influential ethicists take for granted that if something can be done in medicine or the human sciences, it simply should be done, Christian voices that seek a higher ethical standard can be easily cowed. If conventions in academic history strictly limit depictions of the past to what has been determined by economic, political, gender, or ideological forces, Christian historians may flounder in trying to say anything different. If mainline economists treat all human choices as mere calculations of maximized personal advantage, how can believing economists who want to say more respond? If legal scholars, literature professors, or religionists insist upon regarding all human relationships as mere constructions of the human appetite for power, it can be precarious for Christian voices to attempt alternative explanations.

In other words, against the tremendous force of academic convention, it takes a force like Scripture, defined as Baptists have defined it as the fully trustworthy Word of God, to retain a Christian perspective. Moreover, against the power of the academy at large, even a general trust in Scripture will not avail unless scholars have personally appropriated the Bible in the manner that Baptists have always stressed. All academics who long to see a properly authoritative Scripture functioning as a central source of wisdom, direction, insight, guidance, illumination, and inspiration should be grateful to Baptists for insisting on the supremacy of Scripture and to Baptist traditions for defending the rights of individual conscience against the hegemonic control of "worldly powers."

* * *

Yet having an anchor in Scripture amidst the seas of academic turbulence is, of course, only part of the picture. The Baptist history that offers such positive potential for a Christian university has also created real problems, to which we now turn. Significantly, it is important to note that the problems have been there from the beginning. As the histories by David Bebbington and Robert Johnson reveal clearly, once early Baptists went beyond the common approach to baptism itself, the foundational Baptist principles of "soul competency," "religious freedom," "the right of private judgment," and a "gathered church" did not lead to a common theology, common church practices, common attitudes to social engagement, or common approaches to intellectual challenges.

Almost inevitably, the very principles that Baptists shared made it difficult for Baptists to agree among themselves. The fierce determination not to let worldly authorities come between Scripture and the individual believer was matched by a corresponding inability to agree on what Scripture required. And so within less than a century of organized Baptist existence, differences emerged in response to a number of divisive questions and led to the creation of many separate Baptist denominations: Was the atonement universal, as Generals claimed, or specific, as Particulars urged? Should adults who were baptized also receive the laying on of hands? Should the day for public worship be the Sabbath (Saturday) or the first day (Sunday)? Should local leaders accept the validity of adult baptism done elsewhere? Should they require the rebaptism of those who had received infant baptism? Should Baptist fellowships have confessions of faith? Should churches follow Christ's command literally to wash one another's feet? Should Baptists take part in politics or hold aloof? Should conferences of Baptist churches or leaders of those conferences be given any authority within local congregations? For each of these questions, sincere believers in the seventeenth century were able to cite biblical chapters and verses that were completely convincing to themselves—but not to other Baptists. In the centuries since, the number of such questions has multiplied.

For those who think this is a problem only of the deep past, consider more recent Baptist history. Let us imagine that you are a Baptist interested in guidance from other Baptists who, like you, trust in Scripture alone plus conscience alone, on questions about the Bible's most important teachings. Will you line up with the orthodox experientialist E. Y. Mullins, the modernist Harry Emerson Fosdick, the radical Harvey Cox, or the evangelical Carl F. H. Henry? Or let us say you are a Baptist seeking guidance from other Baptists on questions of social responsibility. Would you look to Walter Rauschenbusch, J. Frank Norris, Helen Barrett Montgomery, Martin Luther King, Jr., Will Campbell, or Albert Mohler? Or maybe you seek Baptist counsel on questions about what Christian believers should learn from other religious or intellectual perspectives. Will it be from Shailer Mathews, who was enraptured by the eurekas of modern social science; A. H. Strong, who joined cautious appropriation of evolution to classical Christian orthodoxy; the self-labeled fundamentalist Jerry Falwell, the Calvinist John Piper, or the post-foundationalist James McClendon? Or if you want to describe a classic Baptist approach to American political life, will you find it with Mark Hatfield, Jimmy Carter, Bill Clinton, or Mike Huckabee?

These hypothetical questions underscore the difficulty in moving beyond the Baptist embrace of Scripture plus conscience to even relatively secure perspectives on some of the most important general questions of human existence. The term "Baptist" does define specific attitudes and definite dispositions, but it offers almost no help in defining particular theological, intellectual, or academic stances beyond those attitudes or dispositions. Other Christian traditions also manifest great internal diversity, but Baptists seem to outdo them all. Even for Baptists who have deeply pondered the question, it can be a real puzzle to specify the content that being a Baptist brings to the tasks of academic life.

* * *

If I have described accurately the potential Baptist contribution to academic life, with its firmness on Scripture and conscience, but also the Baptist problem for academic life, with the absence of specific guidance from that firm commitment, how then might a Baptist university maximize the potential of its Baptist heritage while also addressing the problems of that heritage?

There is nothing revolutionary in my recommendations, since what I outline is already taking place at Baylor and other Baptist institutions as well. But it will be a great boon to Christian higher learning more generally for Baptists to be as open and aboveboard as possible about what have already become their best academic practices.

The first step involves pushing back just a little bit from confidence in what my own conscience tells me about how to interpret the Bible. This first step means taking a sobering lesson from the fact that in the United States there exist at least seventy-five Baptist denominations all claiming to follow the Scriptures alone. The appeal is not to abandon the Baptist insistence on soul competency or give up on the right of private judgment. It is rather to keep the dispositions in check that were so admirable in the struggle against tyranny but that now have become intellectually self-defeating in an environment in which tyranny comes more from democratic majorities than from power-wielding despots. Baptist traditions have not been renowned for intellectual humility or a willingness to tolerate intellectual ambiguity. Yet self-denial toward the particularities of one's own individual understanding of Scripture is, for Christian academic life, the only way to go.

A second step is to admit that all interpretations of Scripture, and likewise all academic practices, always depend on traditions of some kind, on conventions that are simply taken for granted, or on unspoken assumptions that no one has thought to challenge. Baptists will know what I'm talking about if they have ever sat in a crowded church in which a rapt congregation seems ready to follow the popular preacher wherever the preacher leads, even if his text concerns the Bereans who, when the Apostle Paul came to town, tested "whether these things are so." It is similar for the ironclad control that unwritten traditions can exert on the worship practices of proudly nonliturgical churches. "Baptist guru," "Baptist kingpin," "Baptist czar," and

"Baptist boss" are all oxymorons, yet you do not have to know a lot of history to be aware of how frequently gurus, kingpins, czars, and bosses have shown up among Baptists.

It is the same for the organization of university life in contemporary America. If we think that our decisions about how to divide intellectual life into departments, or bestow academic credit, or sponsor varsity sports, or organize student housing all spring from exercising the right of private judgment, we delude ourselves. For this second step, self-examination, self-reflection, self-honesty, and a healthy dose of general self-awareness deliver the message that traditions themselves are not the problem. Rather, the real questions concern the character or quality of the traditions that all of us have inherited and that provide substantial structure to much of our lives most of the time.

A third and specifically Christian step for using the Bible productively in academic life is to recognize not only the presence but also the necessity of Christian traditions of biblical interpretation. It can be a difficult lesson for those of us who want to exalt biblical authority over all other authorities to admit that the Bible *per se* does not provide a satisfactory grounding for Christian learning. The Bible *per se* is too easily the source of what Martin Luther called "delusions" that arise when the individual conscience runs wild through the scriptural landscape. It is the narration or message of redemption in the Bible as a whole that can become a satisfactory grounding for Christian learning. For educational purposes, therefore, it is necessary to define the foundational character of Scripture carefully. It is not the Bible alone in any simple sense that can serve as a platform for Christian learning. It is rather the Bible's narrative or story or existential offer of redemption that provides the necessary clarity, depth, and capacity upon which education can be based. The modern Christian university needs a forceful sense of the Bible's message, and not just the Bible alone, as it sets upon its work.

But when we talk about forceful apprehensions of the Bible's message, we are immediately talking about Christian traditions of biblical interpretation that have stood the test of time. In fact, all consequential attempts by believers to use the mind effectively have been grounded in a particular interpretation of the message or narrative of Scripture, rather than simply on the Bible alone. For Catholics there has often been a variety of Thomistic Aristotelianism, for some Calvinists it has been covenant theology, for Lutherans the dialectic of Law and Gospel, for liberal Protestants a systematic deference to modern learning, for Mennonites the principles of nonresistant pacifism, and for the Orthodox a particular reading of humankind in relation to the Incarnation.

Each of the major Christian traditions claims to be biblical, and each offers many illustrations of believers who embrace a particular interpretation of Scripture with the full force of individual conscience. But each one is also more than just simply biblical. The critical question for Christian higher education is not whether such systems exist, but whether the intellectuals who rely on them have made significant contributions that endure and that are obviously Christian. My conclusion is that the best of Christian intellectual life has been nurtured historically within specific Christian traditions marked by two things: first, the "mere Christianity" of the classical creeds, and, second, a productive depth of insight into the human condition or the nature of the universe itself.

Examples can show more clearly what I mean. The best Christian philosophy of the twenty-first century appears in Catholic circles that have been working hard at first-order philosophical problems since the thirteenth century, in Calvinist circles that have been doing the same since the sixteenth century, or from others who have gone to school on the Catholics or the Calvinists. The works of J. S. Bach and Søren Kierkegaard were indeed marked by personal genius, but genius given shape, density, and color by the Lutheran tradition they embraced. Dorothy L. Sayers was a productive novelist, playwright, and critic because she simply had the goods, but also because she practiced an Anglo-Catholic sacramentalism that had been wrestling with aesthetic realities since the late sixteenth century. The anthropologists E. E. Evans-Pritchard, Victor Turner, and Mary Douglas displayed exquisite skill in their ethnographies, but their deepest anthropological insights are unthinkable without considering the Catholic faith that all three practiced. Certainly there has been much good academic work accomplished by Christian believers who are not closely identified with a specific Christian tradition, but not the best work or the work that has been most helpful to other believers.

If by insisting on academic life governed by the Bible alone and the authority of the individual conscience alone Baptists undermine the great Christian traditions, Baptists can be guaranteed to harvest a meager crop of Christian learning.

* * *

In conclusion, I would like to ask how a Baptist university like Baylor, which aspires to be both more Christian and better academically, might move toward an even more productive appropriation of Scripture. In my judgment as a historian and an advocate of Christian intellectual life, a simple Baptist platform has many difficulties. But the feisty, Bible-centered individualism of Baptist tradition does offer an engaging prospect. Baptists have a record of not kowtowing to authority. If Baptists used that spirit of independence to welcome academics from all the major historical Christian traditions who want to prosecute their work by using the deepest insights of their traditions to study the deepest problems of human learning, Baptists would be using the Bible in the contemporary Christian university in just the right way. In addition, if Baptists would actively nurture those scholars, institutes, and programs that tried to show the Christian and academic payoffs from following historical Baptist dispositions, Baptists would be doing a great service to Baptist communities and to American academic life as a whole. And if Baptists demonstrated the traditional Baptist courage in the face of the powers that be—whether those powers are unexamined local traditions, national political enthusiasms, or the conventions of elite American academia—then Baylor University would be doing both Christian and academic worlds the greatest possible service.

Baptists have significant resources that can function like a balance pole on the high wire of modern intellectual life. In Baptist heritage are many examples of fortitude in the face of great opposition. The place of Scripture for the modern Christian university is indeed a problem. But those who understand the life-giving character of the Bible, the wisdom in its pages to orient the tasks of scholarship, and the kind of personal commitment it can inspire are in an excellent place to show the rest of us how to stay on the high wire and not fall off.

NOTES

Davis: Introduction

1. U.S. Census Bureau, Social, Economic, and Housing Statistics Division: Poverty, http://www.census.gov/hhes/www/poverty/about/overview/index.html (last revised September 13, 2011).

2. Ironically, if Harvard historian Niall Ferguson (*Civilization: The West and the Rest* [New York: Penguin, 2011]) is right, China, India, and Brazil will excel precisely because they have adopted Western values and competition precisely when the West is abandoning them.

3. See, for example, John R. Thelin, *A History of American Higher Education*, 2nd ed. (Baltimore: The Johns Hopkins University Press, 2011).

4. Michael Greenstone and Adam Looney, "Where Is the Best Place to Invest $102,000—In Stocks, Bonds, or a College Degree?" The Hamilton Project, The Brookings Institution, June 25, 2011, http://www.brookings.edu/papers/2011/0625_education_greenstone_looney.aspx.

5. Walter Crosby Eells, "Criticisms of Higher Education: Picturesque Exaggerations Found in Current Writings," *Journal of Higher Education* 5, no. 4 (1934): 187.

6. See, especially, Frank Donoghue, *The Last Professors: The Corporate University and the Fate of the Humanities* (New York: Fordham University Press, 2008).

7. Moody's Investors Service, "2011 Outlook for U.S. Higher Education: Stable for Diversified Market Leaders; Negative for Majority of Tuition and State Funding-Dependent Universities," January 14, 2011, http://www.nhhefa.com/documents/moodys2011OutlookforU.S.HigherEducation.pdf.

8   Anthony T. Kronman, *Education's End: Why Our Colleges and Universities Have Given Up on the Meaning of Life* (New Haven: Yale University Press, 2008).

9   One hears in this question the popular work of Jim Collins' *Good to Great: Why Some Companies Make the Leap... and Others Don't* (New York: Harper Collins, 2001).

Elzinga: Christian Higher Education vs. Christians in Higher Education

*   The author is grateful for the comments of Perry L. Glanzer, David L. Jeffrey, and Byron R. Johnson.

1   Abraham Kuyper quotation comes from a speech that he once gave before a university audience in Amsterdam. See Richard J. Mouw, Uncommon Decency (Downers Grove, Ill.: InterVarsity, 1992), 146–47.

2   These professors can be found giving talks to parachurch organizations on their campuses. These professors can be found leading a Bible study in their office with students or other faculty. These professors can be found having office hour conversations about the Christian faith, as well as office hour conversations about their academic disciplines.

3   I am indebted to Frank Smith, who reminded me of Benchley's bifurcation.

4   R. R. Reno, "Schools of Thought," *First Things* (November 2010), 69.

5   As quoted in David S. Dockery and David P. Gushee, *The Future of Christian Higher Education* (Nashville, Tenn.: B&H Publishing, 1999), 19.

6   As quoted in Dockery and Gushee, *The Future of Christian Higher Education*, 117–18.

7   Perry L. Glanzer, "Moving Beyond Value- or Virtue- Added: Transforming Colleges and Universities for Redemptive Moral Development," *Christian Scholar's Review* 39, no. 4, 379–99.

8   Glanzer, "Moving Beyond Value- or Virtue-Added," 392.

9   This is an area where I must bow to Thomas Jefferson, the founder of the University of Virginia. He disliked the academic hierarchy of old world universities. At the then all-male university that he founded, the faculty were to forego all academic titles and simply be called Mr., like the students. To this day, many students at UVA refer to me as "Mr. Elzinga," not "Professor Elzinga" or "Dr. Elzinga."

10   Mark Montgomery, "Confessions of a Bad Academic Advisor," *The Chronicle of Higher Education*, August 8, 2010.

11   Ken Starr, "The Soul of a College," *First Things* (November 2010), 64 (emphasis added).

12   University of Notre Dame (http://www.nd.edu/), The Inauguration of Rev. John I. Jenkins, C.S.C., inaugural address, September 23, 2005, http://inauguration.nd.edu/ceremonies/inaugural_address.shtml.

Elshtain: The Myth of the Sovereign Self

1 Jean Bethke Elshtain, *Sovereignty: God, State, and Self, The Gifford Lectures* (New York: Basic Books, 2008).
2 Albert Camus, *The Rebel* (New York: Vintage Books, 1956), 282–83.
3 Albert Camus, *The First Man*, trans. David Hapgood (New York: Alfred A. Knopf, 1995), 195.
4 Roger Shattuck, *Forbidden Knowledge* (New York: Harcourt, Brace, Vintage Books, 1996), 99.
5 Primo Levi, *Survival in Auschwitz* (New York: Touchstone, 1996), 17, 26, 37, 51, 71.
6 Levi, *Survival in Auschwitz*, 87.
7 Czeslaw Milosz, *The Captive Mind* (New York: Penguin Modern Classics, 2001).
8 Marilynne Robinson, *Gilead* (New York: Farrar, Strauss, & Giroux, 2004), 66, 69.
9 Alistair McFadyen, *Bound to Sin* (Cambridge: Cambridge University Press, 2000), 61, 83.
10 Dietrich Bonhoeffer, *Ethics* (New York: Simon & Schuster, 1995), see 142–64.
11 Dietrich Bonhoeffer, *Creation and Fall* (New York: Macmillan, 1959), 37.
12 Camus, *The Rebel*, 5.
13 Camus, *The Rebel*, 11, 14, 22.
14 Camus, *The Rebel*, 42, 250.
15 Camus, *The Rebel*, 277.
16 Albert Camus, *The Plague* (New York: Vintage International, 1975), 308.

Cantor: Scholarship in Action and the Public Mission of Universities

1 Eugene W. Hilgard, "Progress in Agriculture by Education and Government Aid," *The Atlantic Monthly* 49, no. 294 (April 1882): 531–42, available online at http://cdl.library.cornell.edu/cgi-bin/moa/pageviewer?coll=moa&root=/moa/atla/atla0049/&tif=00537.TIF&view=50&frames=1.
2 See "Brookings Institution Analysis of 'Population of Counties by Decennial Census: 1900 to 1990' (U.S. Census Bureau) and Population Estimates Program Data," and Elizabeth Kneebone and Emily Garr, "Income and Poverty," in State of Metropolitan America: On the Front Lines of Demographic Transformation, a 2010 report by The Brookings Institution, pp. 17 and 132–43, respectively, available online at http://www.brookings.edu/metro/stateofmetroamerica.aspx (accessed 23 November 2010).
3 Ken Starr, "The Soul of a College," *First Things* (November 2010), 62–64.

4   In the 1980s Syracuse led U.S. cities in African American infant deaths. Even now, infants of color die at more than twice the rate of white babies. See the work of medical anthropologist and SU Professor Sandra D. Lane, *Why Are Our Babies Dying? Pregnancy, Birth, and Death in America* (Boulder, Colo.: Paradigm, 2008) for an analysis of structural violence against our most vulnerable citizens.

5   For a recent description of the Genesis project, the work of Luvenia Cowart, a Syracuse University professor and nurse, see James T. Mulder, "Customers Get Health Check and Haircut at Syracuse Barber Shop," The Post-Standard (November 20, 2010), available online at http://blog.syracuse.com/news/print.html?entry=/2010/11/customers_get_health_check_and.html.

6   See the "Statement of The Education Trust on 12th-Grade Reading and Mathematics Results from the 2009 National Assessment of Educational Progress," available online at http://www.edtrust.org/dc/press-room/press-release/statement-of-the-education-trust-on-12th-grade-reading-and-mathematics-r. See also Sarah Almy and Christina Theokas, "Not Prepared for Class: High-Poverty Schools Continue to Have Fewer In-Field Teachers," *The Education Trust*, November 2010, available online at http://www.edtrust.org/dc/publication/not-prepared-for-class-high-poverty-schools-continue-to-have-fewer-in-field-teachers.

7   The Syracuse City School District, "District Demographics and Profile," available online at http://www.syracusecityschools.com/?q=node/828 (accessed November 20, 2010).

8   Quotations are from a speech delivered at the 11th annual convention of the Southern Christian Leadership Conference, Atlanta, Georgia, August 16, 1967.

Shulman: The Challenges and Opportunities for Liberal Education in a Faith-Based University

1   I have explored this set of ideas more fully in my essay "Professing Understanding and Professing Faith: The Midrashic Imperative," in *The American University in a Postsecular Age*, ed. Douglas Jacobsen and Rhonda Husted Jacobsen, 203–17 (New York: Oxford University Press, 2008).

2   Robert D. Putnam and David E. Campbell, *American Grace: How Religion Divides and Unites Us* (New York: Simon & Schuster, 2010).

3   Anne Colby, Thomas Ehrlich, William M. Sullivan, and Jonathan R. Dolle, *Rethinking Undergraduate Business Education: Liberal Learning for the Profession* (San Francisco: Jossey-Bass, 2011).

4   Charles R. Foster, Lisa E. Dahill, Lawrence A. Golemon, and Barbara Wang Tolentino, *Educating Clergy: Teaching Practices and Pastoral Imagination* (San Francisco: Jossey-Bass, 2006).

5   Eli Gottlieb and Sam Wineburg, "Between *Veritas* and *Communitas*: Epistemic Switching in the Reading of Academic and Sacred History," *The*

Journal of the Learning Sciences (2011), now available online, DOI 10.1080/ 10508406.2011.582376.

6 The observation that Professor B is Christian and Professor C is Jewish should not lead us to conclude that the modes of thought each exhibits are characteristically Christian or Jewish as such. With two other historians these two forms of switching could well be reversed.

7 Lee S. Shulman, *Teaching as Community Property: Essays on Higher Education* (San Francisco: Jossey-Bass, 2004).

Noll: The Bible, Baptists, and the Challenge of Christian Higher Education

1 This lecture adapts material on the Reformation first published in my articles "The Place of Scripture in the Modern University," Valparaiso University's *The Cresset*, Trinity 2011 (vol. 74, no. 5): 6–15; and "So You're a Baptist: What Might That Mean?" *Books & Culture* (July/August 2011): 9–10, discussing the recent Baptist histories by Robert E. Johnson and David Bebbington.

2 "Luther at the Diet of Worms," trans. Roger A. Hornsby, in *Luther's Works*, vol. 32: *Career of the Reformer II*, ed. George W. Forell (Philadelphia: Fortress, 1958), 111 (emphasis added).

3 "Luther at the Diet of Worms," 112.

4 "Luther at the Diet of Worms," 113.

5 "Preface to the New Testament," trans. Charles M. Jacobs, in *Luther's Works*, vol. 35: *Word and Sacrament I*, ed. E. Theodore Bachman (Philadelphia: Fortress, 1960), 357.

6 Robert E. Johnson, *A Global Introduction to Baptist Churches* (New York: Cambridge University Press, 2010); David W. Bebbington, *Baptists through the Centuries: A History of a Global People* (Waco, Tex.: Baylor University Press, 2010).

7 William H. Brackney, "Baptists, Religious Liberty and Evangelization: Nineteenth-Century Challenges," in *Baptist Identities*, ed. I. M. Randall, T. Pilli, and A. R. Cross (Eugene, Ore.: Wipf & Stock, 2006), 325.

8 "Comparison of 1925, 1963, and 2000 Baptist Faith and Message," website of the Southern Baptist Convention, http://www.sbc.net/bfm/bfmcomparison.asp.